Ecstasy: Case Unsolved

In the same series
The Case Against Hysterectomy
Sandra Simkin
The Case for Taking the Date out of Rape
Aileen McColgan

Ecstasy: Case Unsolved

SHEILA HENDERSON

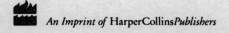

An Imprint of HarperCollins*Publishers*

Pandora
An Imprint of HarperCollins*Publishers*
77–85 Fulham Palace Road
Hammersmith, London W6 8JB

Published by Pandora 1997

1 3 5 7 9 10 8 6 4 2

A catalogue record for this book
is available from the British Library

ISBN 0 04 440917 6

Printed and bound in Great Britain by
Caledonian International Book Manufacturing Ltd, Glasgow

To Aeon and Zoë

Contents

Acknowledgements ix

Introduction xi

PART 1: THE BACKGROUND

1   It takes two (generations) to tango 3

PART 2: THE CASE

2   The case so far 15

3   Fear, ease and beyond 30

4   Drugs 'r' us: the slippery slope 43

5   Sex, drugs and the modern girl 65

6   Chemical culture and modern manhood 87

PART 3: THE CONCLUSION

7   Ecstasy: case unsolved 111

Bibliography 127

Acknowledgements

The ideas in this book have been sampled and remixed from far too many sources to mention by name. However, particular thanks are due to Jane Collins and Rachel Thomson for their support, ideas, comments, great dinners and much, much more; to Rod Henderson for the same but for bearing the additional burden of living with me while I was continually tied to a computer; to friends and colleagues who helped with the research/commented on drafts/taught me a great deal and made it fun along the way: Sean Arnold, Fran Beckett, Andrew Bennett, Kerry Blair, Joe Blair, Wendy Blair, Hannah Collins, Michelle Durkin, Mark Gilman, Mike Linnell, Alan Matthews, Janette Matthews, Sean Nixon, Jacqui Pretty, Nigel South, Nicky Tansley, Lindsey and Rob Vasey, Trevor Wadlow; to all the young Brits who have been so willing to chat; to the North West Regional Health Authority and the Home Office for funding all my research (and whose views this book does not represent); to all the songwriters whose tunes I have played around with; to Sara Dunn and the team at Pandora for being so patient; and last but by no means least, to Zoë and Aeon Henderson for their support, comments and tolerance of a parent interested in their generation.

Introduction

I have been making my living from illegal drugs for a few years now. Or, phrased less loosely, as a social researcher I have undertaken quite a few projects on the subject in a number of areas of Britain on behalf of government departments, drug advice and counselling agencies and charities. I have stood on conference platforms in this country and abroad heralded as a drug 'expert' (although if you expect me to display a laddish, trainspotting approach to drugs, all pharmacology and the latest street names, you might be disappointed). The words I have written and spoken on the subject must be close to acquiring six zeros. Look in the Who's Who of research on illegal drugs and you may find me. But that's not the only reason I'm writing this book. While my work has taught me a few things about contemporary youth drug culture and, I suppose, given me some authority to speak, it would be cowardly to hide behind the veil of dispassionate 'expertise' while pronouncing on a subject so saturated in morality and passion. Of course my research informs what I have to say but without the reference points of my own personal experience as a girl growing up in the fifties and sixties and as a parent since the seventies, what I know and feel about it would be minimal.

The funny thing about drugs is that so many people who live a lifestyle in which drugs play a part don't think drugs are a problem, while the people who don't live the lifestyle, declaim drugs (often very loudly). Even funnier is that, when it comes to today's recreational drug use especially, so many of the users are under 35 and so many abstainers and declaimers are well over the 30-something hill. Perhaps what is not so funny is that, on this other side of the hill, there appears to be so little actual understanding of or desire to understand contemporary youth drug culture. At least you would think so to judge by the level of public debate. Paul Betts, father of the young woman who died after taking Ecstasy in November 1995 and, along with his wife, a key public figure since that time, put his finger on it in a recent interview with one of the biggest selling 'Dance music and club culture' magazines, *Mixmag*. He summed up the predominant generational relationship around drugs well when he described the problem in modern society as being that 'we wrinklies don't know anything about your generation. We talk a lot of twat and twaddle.' (Headon, 1996a).

This book is about what happened when the drug-full-of-promise called Ecstasy got together with dance/house music and youthful dancing in Britain after dark. An increasingly global phenomenon, what has variously been called 'Acid House', 'rave', 'dance culture', 'club culture', the 'chemical generation', (and what I aim to call culturE, out of laziness) is frequently claimed to involve one million young people every weekend in Britain. It's been behind what the sociologists used to call a moral panic which has been sweeping Britain in waves since the late eighties and you would have to have been pot-holing, astronauting or religious culting for a very long time to know nothing about it. But this book is about more than any simple attack on or defence of a drug or of the cultures it helped to define. I happen to think that such a project is both impossible in 1997 and futile, although that seems to be what generally happens when Ecstasy is discussed. This book is about the growth of a significant culture, a lifestyle, and the fear and loathing that surrounds it. It's about identifying the fear of the unknown and the confusion it stirs in the adult population in Britain, and the flipside state of ease this fear itself produces on the other side of the generational divide. It's about the different things Ecstasy came to symbolise to Planets Youth and Middle Age towards the end of a century and how this generational dynamic helped fuel a new chemical culture. In short, it is about exploring the Ecstasy case from a different angle. It is about forgetting to ask 'what's to be done?' for a while. It is about stopping the usual search for solutions and trade in certainties which are the mainstay of the Ecstasy case – and following a different line of inquiry.

My aim in this book is to move the inter-generational and inter-lifestyle dialogue around drugs beyond 'twat and twaddle', beyond the false polarity which debate around drugs inevitably falls into in Britain and globally. Only a short, sharp yank against the twin poles of prohibition and libertarianism can begin to bridge the huge generation/lifestyle gap which exists in this and many other countries, and move us beyond war or peace, getting tough or tender, condemning or condoning drugs and onto safer ground. So I intend to move and shake a few of your assumptions, be you young or old, pro-, con- or just indifferent to the much-hyped youth phenomenon that is culturE. I can hear the yawning now, such is the media overload on all things young, druggy and sexy – but hear me out. It is impossible to avoid morality altogether in this morally overcharged area of debate but I'm going to try to avoid getting too bogged down in the persistent questions – should we bang up all the drug users and the dealers, should we legalise, etc. That ground is currently caught in a loop and we need to switch if off for a while and play a different tune.

No, what I want to do is to take a fresh look at the Ecstasy case. Open it up, leave certainty behind and take you on a series of short flights, not of fancy but into a set of differing realities on both sides of the Ecstasy hill. Then we can go beyond the generational divide and see where it leads us. Drugs may well be, in the recent words of the Chief Constable of West Yorkshire Police (on BBC2's *Public Eye* programme, 'Beyond the drugs war'), 'choking the criminal justice system' and 'at the heart of the politics of this country' but I aim to concentrate more on looking at drugs for the cultures and lifestyles they and the responses to them are a part of. I do, of course, run the risk of being attacked from all sides but that is one more risk-taking activity I choose to participate in.

MY GENERATION YOUR GENERATION

Why bother to attempt to bridge the generation gap? After all, it is part of the human condition, surely? At least, it has been in Britain since the Never-Had-It-So-Good years after the Second World War when the concept of 'youth' was invented and the fires of inter-generational fear and loathing were fanned. Music, style, drugs and dancing in the dark have often featured as a generational wedge in the West and the clash between socially-sanctioned versus socially-demonised cultures involving drug-taking is by no means new. It is perhaps hard to imagine now but modern ballroom dancing was once cause for alarm to the British public, as well as the arrivals of jive and rock 'n' roll.

Modern ballroom dancing may easily degenerate into a sensuous form of entertainment, and if self-control is weakened with alcohol it is more than likely that it will do so, which might easily lead at least to unruly behaviour and not infrequently to sexual immorality.
ENGLISH LIFE AND LEISURE, 1951 (QUOTED IN EVERITT, 1986).

The film was stopped for 18 minutes, in the hope that the uproar among the audience of 900 would subside, but each time one of the 'rock and roll' bands interrupted the story of the film with the first manic whine of a saxophone, boys leapt from the front stalls into the front aisle and stamped their suede shoes in the octopus whirling of jive. Young people at the back of the cinema, when they were not training fire hoses, gave vent to their emotion by stretching their arms out to the screen like savages drunk with coconut wine at a tribal sacrifice.
A SCREENING OF THE BLACKBOARD JUNGLE WHICH FEATURED 'ROCK AROUND THE CLOCK' REPORTED IN THE MANCHESTER GUARDIAN, 1956 (QUOTED IN EVERITT, 1986).

We danced as no boy or girl ever did before. The clamour of drums and bass beat through our blood, sweeping us on in a fury of motion.
ON THE JITTERBUG (QUOTED IN MORIARTY, 1979).

And so on through the jealous world of post-war youth cults. You name it, drugs, music, style and dancing have played an integral, hedonistic part. Actually, there were youth, style, drugs and music scares well before the teenage consumer was born too. The tango and jazz in the years after the Great War are just one example.

Our Tango madness. The death agonies of the dance? Among the cultured youth of America, who seemed crazed by quest of jazz and pleasure ... The wild beats of jazz, syncopated to the pulsations of the heart, exact as terrible a penalty from the nerves as does a drug...
(QUOTED IN SILVA, 1979).

INTRODUCTION

> They say the nightclubs are opening up in rows, and dressmakers say they're
> dizzy with the orders for dance frocks that keep pourin' in. And they just
> can't have enough niggers to play jazz music, and I hear are thinkin' of
> hiring out squads of 'loonies' to make the mad jazz noises till there are more
> ships 'vailable to bring the best New York 'musicians' over.
>
> THE TATLER, 1919 (QUOTED IN KOHN, 1992).

> [My] companion pointed out three girl-addicts to cocaine. One was a frail-
> looking creature about twenty in a flimsy frock that left three-quarters of her
> back bare. During the intervals of her vivacious dancing in an underground
> room, she gave herself over to almost hysterical attacks of inane, purposeless
> laughter, and now and then stroked the man sitting with her.
>
> THE EVENING NEWS, 1922 (QUOTED IN KOHN, 1992).

This RAF serviceman's description of his peers dancing during
the Second World War bears an uncanny resemblance to modern
descriptions of 'raves' in some ways (although the live band/vocalist
and boy/girl couple dancing format was different):

> A smoke-hazed aeroplane hangar 'somewhere in England', the floor crowded
> to capacity with uniformed boys and girls swaying or 'jiving' wildly
> according to the dictates of that essential commodity, the dance band, the
> vocalist ... singing of love not war ... The dance was on and all we were
> conscious of was the music (and what music it was) and the exhilarating
> rhythm and of course the girl on our arm.
>
> (QUOTED IN COSTELLO, 1985).

Youthful hedonism and defiance of what went before, of the
world order elders have helped create, may now seem like an integral
part of the modern condition; they usually are. But today's
generational rift is about more than just the inevitable. Each youth
phenomenon appears on a particular historical landscape, has its

own specific economic, cultural and political recipe. The phenomenon which was first 'Acid House', and has grown, diversified and continually mutated, drawing in predominantly people born in the three decades from the sixties to the eighties to date, is a story of youth in our post-modern times. A story in which young people living on the tiny island which introduced the world to the stiff upper lip and work ethic, appear to be dedicated to pleasure and altered mind states. In a Britain devastated by poverty, unemployment and urban decay, characterised by a growing gap between rich and poor, educated and near-illiterate, healthy and ill-cared-for sick (of the mental as well as physical kind), the expectations and aspirations of young and old, young people want it all – at least for the moment. Pleasure, fun, travel, happiness, money even. Weaned on the adage that 'there is no such thing as society', the *me* generation has striven to find a way to be the *we* generation, a way of belonging, something to belong to. All aspirations and few options, it is hardly surprising that, in stories of contemporary youth, the cradle so often now leads to (what used to be called) the 'rave'.

Time was that youth was a (brief) period of irresponsibility between childhood and adulthood but now the goalposts of life, its rites of passage, have changed. Time was you got an education, left school or university, got a job, married and settled down, now this straightforward narrative (never the full story) is fading. Time was you knew your place in society as a man or a woman, now women have begun to get some of the things they envied men for and they are not altogether sure they want them. Meanwhile, men have (often involuntarily) given up a lot of things they had and are left dazed and confused or bloody-minded. Time was you *could* get through your youth without being offered illegal drugs, now that chance is slim. Time was you *could* have sex without wading through an ocean, rather than a mere stream of warnings that it could make you die a horrible death. Time was that most nightclubs closed at midnight,

2am at the latest, now you can club all through the weekend. CulturE, a hybrid if ever there was one, has so far defied the perennial proclamations of its demise and threatens to carry the youth party through to the end of the twentieth century.

The huge gap between this 'party' and the (disintegrating) lifestyles of a bygone age may never be bridged. And maybe trying to do so is a waste of time. But Leah Betts' media death and her parents' continued high profile did something to that gap. Among other things, it opened the eyes of many over the Ecstasy hill to what had been going on under their noses more than ever before. They may not understand it, they may not even want to, but if there was ever a time when bridging the gap enough to make a difference was even vaguely possible, it could be now. What is more, a more significant proportion of people over 35 years of age will now, more than ever before in Britain, have had some (past or current) kind of (direct or indirect) experience of a recreational drug culture in a consumer-based society. They're in a minority but a growing one. Being part of this minority in itself is no guarantee of or passport to understanding culturE, getting real about it or not trying to control or own it. However, combined with the good old retro-values of honesty and common sense, it *may* just predispose the numerous individuals concerned to a more realistic view. They may recall, or still live, elements of lifestyle which have been incorporated into today's far from homogeneous chemical culture. They may have also moved with the times enough to empathise or simply communicate with contemporary youth lifestyles. Enough to accept some responsibility for the world as it is today even, instead of blaming the world's inheritors. They may still live in the real world instead of a fantasy island of fifties English culture, all warm beer and cricket flannels.

CHARTERING EXCURSIONS BETWEEN PLANETS YOUTH AND MIDDLE AGE

Some members of this minority have made the voyage to Planet Youth in recent years and decided to invade. Or, as the 'hip' youth magazine, *Mixmag*, put it in a feature on 'over-40s ravers' early in 1996, have put 'one foot in the rave' (Headon, 1996a). Opinion on these aged ones, courted and reported in the feature, demonstrated that the urge to maintain a generation gap can be as strong from the other side. This 21-year-old man was not alone in his opinion that:

> *Basically, it's pretty fucking sad seeing someone pilled up at that age. They should be in an office or tied to a sink or something. It's not their generation's music, anyway, it's ours. They should be listening to glam rock or punk or something.*
> (QUOTED IN HEADON, 1996B)

But it also suggested a departure from the jealousy of youth cults and an openness to inter-generational hedonism which the men in the feature themselves reported experiencing. Take the opinion of this 25-year-old woman:

> *It's quite hopeful really to think that people of that age can enjoy themselves and can go out and mix with people our age.*
> (QUOTED IN HEADON, 1996A)

The predominance of this view was confirmed in a later issue of the magazine, which reported being inundated with letters supporting the 'oldies', who had become 'club celebs' (*Mixmag*, 1996a). It is an opinion I have come across many times before. I have encountered it in the many interviews I've conducted around the country when asking about the average age of particular venues or 'scenes'. ('Granny E', a 62-year-old raver known to some young interviewees in the North West in the late eighties, was just one of the more memorable older 'characters' drawn to my attention.) I have encountered it when the 'wrinklie ravers' I have met have recounted their experiences. I have encountered it in the obvious respect among young people for the information material on drugs produced by the few 30- and 40-something drug education professionals who bother to connect with culturE and communicate in its own terms. I have encountered it when, because of the rapport we had established, interviewees have (mistakenly) assumed I'm a one-foot-in-the-raver myself. I have also seen it on documentaries.

It is also obvious from the popularity of the books on Ecstasy by Nicholas Saunders, one-time 'Alternative London'er, Neal's Yard entrepreneur and, at 50-something, originally interested in Ecstasy for its use in psychotherapy. He is now hailed as the 'Buddha of Euphoria' or 'a Timothy Leary for the nineties' and respected for his quest to fill the vacuum of knowledge about the drug (Bellos, 1995). Timothy Leary himself, the High Priest of sixties counter-culture, has been revered by the new chemical generation and went clubbing via virtual space before he died. The biochemist, Alexander Shulgin – 'stepfather' of the drug which came to be known as Ecstasy, MDMA – is another wrinkly well respected. Think too, of Michael Eavis, veteran patron saint of the now internationally-renowned Glastonbury festival. CJ Stone, of The Guardian's 'Housing Benefit Hill' column fame, has recently written of the counter-cultural 'Fierce Dancing' of the new chemical generation and tours the dancefloors of Britain after dark reading it (Stone, 1996). Even Irvine Welsh, literary guru of the new chemical generation, is, at 38, on the launchpad for Planet Middle Age (although he has been rumoured to be older).

This form of inter-generational contact, this acceptance of and respect for actual visitors or heroes from Planets Middle and Old Age among some of the youth of today (as opposed to their symbolic reworking of past youth cults galore) is probably not a major phenomenon. The proportion of 'wrinklies' who knew a good thing when they saw it, dived in and stayed there must be even more minimal. But it is a phenomenon nonetheless and its (partial, at least) acceptance by the younger generation is telling. Contrast it with the fear and loathing of culturE we have grown accustomed to in a media with youth-amnesia.

Contrast it also with the complacency of the guardians of youth cults past. A number of individuals have made a day excursion to Planet Youth and returned with a sneer on their staunchly anti-consumerist faces. To them, today's youth present a weak and pallid imitation of themselves in former years. Take this *Guardian* writer's comparison of her own experience of Glastonbury 25 years previously with the one she witnessed in 1994:

> A Tor. A knot of fields. Stages. Music. Another 100,000 people ... Another world – at first neither recognised nor remembered. You walk around in growing dismay. This is nothing to do with peace and love. This is alien. Hostile. Horrible ... What have they done to what we did? Only the toilets remain the same ... Our old acid-casualty friends must be turning in their graves. The breadheads have taken over ... and delivered unto us a parody of the loving times where much of it looks the same and little of it is. The clothes are still tie-dyed ... sold by the ton at ludicrous prices ... all the stallholders are happy to take credit cards ... The greed is everywhere ... All of a sudden, a funny thing happened ... The sun shone ... and time, 25 years of it, suspended itself. The same emotional camaraderie gripped as if it had never slackened; we were lost in the full-throated roar of recognition ... The sound systems have come on a pace since 1969. As long as the sun does shine and as long as the music does play, there is sharing after all. As soon as you realise that, your heart opens to a few more good things ... None of this adds up to revolution, but perhaps at Glastonbury I found our legacy after all: a generation that, for all its faults, is that bit nicer, more

caring and more loving than it might have been if it had not been for us.
That'll do. For now.

(SARLER, 1994)

CONFESSIONS OF A TRAVEL AGENT

So who am I to step into the breach, to try and develop this inter-planetary and inter-polar tourism? Well, I'm not a hip young thing totally clued up on the club, music and fashion scenes. I'm definitely not Granny (or even auntie) 'E' or a 'one foot in the grave' raver and I have no designs upon becoming the High Priestess of Euphoria. I'm not a sad, bad old adolescent, 'Absolutely Fabulous' or even just sad. I can't afford to take drugs in my line of work, even if I wanted to. However, I did go to festivals before Glastonbury was invented, which means I *am* currently participating in an activity recently described as 'more devastating than drink, drugs and divorce' (Neustatter, 1996). It is a widespread pursuit, a quarter of Europeans and 21 per cent of Americans are also supposedly involved, to name but a few. It's called mid-life. The thing I thought I'd die before I got. The thing that looked awful cold from the heat of youth. It involves wrestling with mid-body expansion, wrinkles, greying hair, lack of energy, sexual invisibility, empty nest syndrome, overheating, the big life questions like 'What have I achieved?', 'What future is there?', 'When can I go shopping/have a holiday?', that kind of thing. I seem to have evolved from Twiggy to Miss Piggy almost overnight and getting into a pair of hipsters is just not what it used to be. I have two offspring in their twenties, a mortgage, a career of sorts, I live in a little house in the country.

If I could, I'd try and minimise the risks and harms of this devastating activity and settle for drink, drugs or divorce instead but the bright colours of the summer of my life are giving way to mists and mellow fruitfulness whether I like it or not. Actually, mostly I like it. Truism it may be but I'm more at home with myself than I've ever been. But, call me immature or tell me to butt my aging body out of things that don't concern me, I do take a healthy interest in what is happening on Planet Youth (and it's not just because my kids are there). I like to have some idea, however minimal, of how the social and cultural landscape is shaping up for another century. I have not forgotten my own time on the planet but I don't guard it jealously or try to muscle in, Peter Pan-like, and re-colonise it. I am a great believer in a respectful generation *distance*, rather than a generation *gap*ing hole. Perhaps I'm an aspiring inter-generational envoy, an interpreter specialising in the translation of 'twat and twaddle'. But, then again, I'm definitely not Janet Street-Porter.

It's typical, of course, that yet another old duffer is pronouncing on things youthful. It seems to be the only thing the official world will allow. Even though there are plenty of what you'd think are 'public' youthful voices – for instance, magazines (due to the size and nature of their circulation). However, they pass the majority of the adult world by. Sad isn't it that, once the cellulite kicks in and the oestrogen needs replacing by either determination or alternative chemical means, the over-the-hill need to pronounce on things elastic and resilient, all future and little past. But this, it would seem, is life. I can't get away from the fact that I'm yet another wrinkly pronouncing on everything that figures in the lives of another generation, from 'Coronation Street' to politics. But at least my attempt is a bit different. At least I'm not a dude pretending to be cool while struggling with nose hair, bushy eyebrows, a decline in my pulling power and, basically, in danger of becoming a sad old git.

Not like most of the public voices of the post-war generations in Britain that have embraced illicit substances as an alternative route to putting a finger up to the established world while finding their own way. Especially those who've pronounced on culturE. They've all lent a specifically male definition to things chemically non-mainstream.

If, like Irvine Welsh's male character, Ally, in 'An Acid House Romance' (Welsh, 1996a), you're dismissive of those into things 'straight-peg', 'all that home and garden shite', then you're not cool. At least, not if you're a bloke. The domestic sphere of everyday practicality, portrayed as 'bourgeois' in my day, has always had a greater hold on women. Even at their most bohemian. Whether they wash them or not, girls still seem to get faced with a pile of dishes at least two weeks old or a stinky toilet bowl, in a way the boys rarely seem to. The same applies to waking up to a bun in the proverbial oven. So at least my voice is a different one. My youth was (mis?)spent on society's margins, exploring a way of life more meaningful to me than a nine-to-five means of filling my own and my family's mouth. And I haven't forgotten it. In fact, if I had to choose, I am, like journalist Suzanne Moore, 'on the side of youth, not because older people have nothing to contribute but because they have had their chance to contribute' (Moore, 1996).

I *am* a product of the sixties but I've kept my mind open since. There are a lot of us 'wrinklies' out here who did inhale in the sixties, who dare to admit we once wore 'ding-a-ling' trousers and preached love and peace even though we came to be deeply embarrassed by it all in the eighties. Especially when punk's heavy-booted kick in the teeth of hippiedom finally filtered through to our adolescent kids in the shape of Neil, the daft hippy's, vilification in *The Young Ones* on TV. We were truly in the stocks on Dodgy Youth Culture village green with egg all over our faces but they've found some things our era was good for now and added it to the heady remix which is their own. Meanwhile, we've learnt to cringe when our own generation reveres the sixties. It took humiliation to let the wind out of our pride. We don't lay claim to ownership of all that has ever been authentic about youth culture but we haven't thrown the baby out with the bathwater of youth – even though we have paid our taxes, had careers, looked after our families, voted and cared about the society we live in. As parents, we tried to encourage caring and sharing values in our children, to help them develop their own sense of right and wrong, to think for themselves. Even though society was pulling us all the other way. Look after number one, step over anyone to get to the top, to get the big car, big house, big stereo, big hair. This was the culture our kids grew up in outside the home. We've all had to accommodate to a brave new world, gaining our identity increasingly through consumption and making our way through the jungle. We're good citizens in many ways, professionals even, but we still have a sense of humour and haven't lost a taste for music, looking good and enjoying ourselves. We don't necessarily need the sun to shine and the band to play all the time to recognise the good in those who will inherit the earth.

What is more, 'wrinklies' who cut their youth cultural teeth in the sixties and seventies abound in today's professions. Some still maintain their links to today's burgeoning unofficial worlds. The drugs service, policy and research field is full of them, although refugees from ensuing youth cultures have contributed and continue to swell the ranks, along with a good contingent who would not know a youth culture if it jumped up and hugged them, spat at them or pushed a broken bottle in their face. It has to be said that there is still a strong whiff of original sandals and patchouli oil in some quarters – even under the skin of eighties power dressing or the faded downwardly-mobile attire of the academy. After all, as a long-time director of Manchester's Lifeline, once one of the biggest drug agencies in the country, put it, the early voluntary drug services were 'the field hospitals of the counter-culture revolution. Some ... remained behind after the armistice was declared to care for the wounded, the displaced and the lonely' (Yates, 1992). But there is also a smattering of individuals who, like myself, know cKOne ('The first unisex fragrance of the new generation'. 'The fragrance that can adapt to, rather than dictate, their moods') when we smell it and duck and dive our way through professionalism and personal trauma, principle and pragmatism, humour and despair, authoritarianism and libertarianism.

I'm a bit of an an interloper into this corner of a professional world. Although more than one of us was a mature student, a 'late-starter', the other professional 'old youth' are old lads every one. They are the true drug experts. They live and breathe drugs. Know every pharmacological name and fact there is to know, what's happening on the streets. They Internet their knowledge and use their expertise to influence the policy-makers and to inform and advise young people and parents about drugs. I'm in the research-for-policymaking business too but I'm interested in drugs as part of a cultural and social mix, as a reflection of wider social change, as a way of defining identity, more than anything. An interest aided and abetted by a bent for looking to history to make sense of the present, together with a passing romance with that strange academic discipline called Cultural Studies.

Nonetheless, unlike a lot of 'old youth' who were so protective of their 'original', we (these drug experts and myself) saw in the early days of culturE what many of today's youth saw – what we thought to be a greater democratisation of youth culture than we had ever witnessed in mod, hippy, punk or soccer casual heaven or anything since. Black/white, male/female, gay/straight, whatever social class, north/south, urban/rural, able-bodied/disabled, it all seemed not to matter. Jaded from years of political defeat and still blinking with disbelief as we witnessed the devastation of all we held dear socially, it was balm which soothed its way through a hard shell of cynicism. As parents, we were relieved that our little gems, if they had to make their way through youth cultures perennially fraught with risk and danger, would at least have to negotiate one devoted to pleasure but seemingly so egalitarian, so free of aggression, violence and sexual danger and so devoted to togetherness and empathy ... It was a romantic vision but, although, right now, it is much easier to return to dark cynicism as an old youth and to fear as a parent – as the 'jungle' that is now much of Britain is an inescapable fact, in nightclubs, warehouses and fields as anywhere – something has been afoot. So forget asking 'what is to be done?' for a while. Stop getting caught up in the endless cycle of discussing, or watching discussions about, whether Ecstasy is good or bad. Stop worrying about it or being blasé about it for a while. Stop being so publicly certain, give in to those nagging uncertainties and follow me into a new line of inquiry into the Ecstasy case. One which won't offer you any easy solutions but which will at least get you thinking about some of the cultural, economic and social changes Ecstasy has become symbolic of.

PART 1

The Background

1

It takes two
(generations) to tango

The nation first woke up to Acid House with the morning
cornflakes in 1988. The tabloids heralded a 'groovy' new youth cult.
The quality press documented it. 'News at Ten' poked gentle fun at it.
Here was simply the latest in a long line of fads which were the
inevitable lot of every generation in their youth. Or, in the words of a
Sunday Times article at the time:

> *Every generation finds its cult. And when Acid House arrived in London*
> *earlier this year, to the thousands of adolescents who had not been part of*
> *one before, it was perfect. It came complete with its own music, its own strict*
> *dress codes, a brand new drug called Ecstasy and, most importantly of all,*
> *the promise of a good time.*
>
> (PRAGNELL, 1988)

Dancing all night to loud repetitive music in a dark space
crammed with sweating bodies may not be a particularly new youth

leisure pursuit. It may also hold little promise of pleasure for many over the age of 35. But when 'Acid House' made its public debut in Britain with tabloid images of ecstatic young people dancing trance-like en masse, this youthful nocturnal pursuit was taking rather a new turn. The size of the nocturnal social space occupied by young people increased beyond anything witnessed before: the vast numbers attending some events have made a school disco out of what many a parent knew as a large packed club in their day. Meanwhile, although nightclubs played their usual role, events also took place in fields, old warehouses and other decaying monuments to a bygone industrial age. Leisure centres and other temples of the modern consumer age also got a look in. Particularly motorway services. A far cry from the Palais, Ritzy's and Roxy's of various yesteryears of youth.

And then there was the music. Many a mum and dad may even have made merry in the mud and dug the vibes in fields at festivals, wedged damply but deliriously among thousands of others. But the music was not like this before. Now it emitted from powerful sound systems and rattled through your body and mind at a rate of 120 repetitive beats per minute. And just to underline the leisure status of this mass elation, loud and proud, brightly-coloured clothes you were more likely to spot on a Spanish holiday were its early trademark. What is more, devotees paid significantly more than the price of entrance to a drink-dance-and-grope night for the pleasure; stretched Saturday night into a whole weekend; and, like dedicated football supporters, were prepared to travel to 'somewhere in Britain' (or even the world), which often required well-developed orienteering skills to reach. And finally, the drugs. One in particular. As illegal as heroin in the eyes of the law but initially viewed as harmless by its users: Ecstasy (or Methylenedioxyamphetamine, MDMA, if you want to get technical; somewhere between LSD and amphetamine if you don't) enhanced youth's nocturnal party like no other drug. Hedonism and 'luvdup' bonding on a grand scale became a social phenomenon more mass than the hippies 'love-ins' ever were. Perhaps not unsurprisingly, this weekend 'holiday' from the everyday humdrum of *fin de siècle* British life (from which some have refused to return), has been great cause for public concern over the intervening decade.

To note these changes in things youthful is to only begin to tell the story of music, dance and drugs culture in these post-modern times. Despite many attempts by the official world to control or crush it and perennial announcements made by 'hip' youth that the phenomenon has finally died, the music and culture associated with the use of Ecstasy and other dance drugs not only continues to survive, it is a growing cultural phenomenon which, for large numbers of Britons born between 1961 and 1982 in particular (but by no means exclusively), provides a social reference point which is difficult to ignore. It's a cultural phenomenon which does not name itself, and certainly not specifically through use of the drug, Ecstasy. And, although it was small, elite, relatively homogeneous and 'subcultural' in the early days, culturE fragmented into a hydra of different subscenes long ago, and continues to do so. Some are happily part of mainstream popular culture, some determinedly out in the margins and many converge in a largescale meeting ground in between. All are increasingly divided along lines of age, sexuality, race, class and defined by a specific type of music, social identity and codes of dress, dancing and general etiquette: Jungle, hardcore, acid jazz, garage, trance, house, bhangra, to name but a few among the myriad.

The combination of Ecstasy (and now a much wider range of drug) use, all-night dancing and music, loosely termed 'dance' or 'house', remains a central cultural activity for a wide range of young Britons (frequently claimed to figure as high as one million every week). If nothing else, it's a means of spending the weekend. But it's also a kind of cultural currency, a means of gaining identity, of giving life meaning and value (even if any or all these are achieved in defining yourself in opposition to the phenomenon). It is a means of differentiating or aligning oneself from/with parents/older generations, other young people and other social groups, whether you actually buy into it wholeheartedly and dance the night away or not. Because as well as being a cultural phenomenon which has seen young people claiming social spaces for their use – fields, warehouses, sports stadia, aircraft hangars, holiday camps etc – like never before, it has also made a huge impact on the mainstream. All the cultural industries associated with 'youth' – music, fashion, drugs, nightclubs (and now, the café-bar) – have been irrevocably affected, causing annual turnovers to boom. But it doesn't end there. It has spread far beyond them, providing advertisers with a whole new lifestyle to target. And, while the signs of the culture went undetected in many ways in the official world, they have been increasingly everywhere. Its music now soundtracks everything from football and other sports coverage and kids' TV programmes to holiday and travel programmes, you name it. Watch TV or a movie at the cinema and the chances are, in 1996, you'll see ice-creams, fizzy drinks and new telephone companies, at the very least, being advertised by young people, music and visual and verbal references obviously identifiable with the new chemical culture.

The story of this cultural transformation is long and complicated. To trace its origins would be the work of several lifetimes. One thing is for sure, this cultural phenomenon didn't just spring from nowhere (and it isn't acknowledged by many young participants eager to maintain a distinct identity). It was certainly a product of youth keen to do what youth have frequently done in a consumer society – define themselves against the establishment, the older generation. There is also no doubt that different youth groups wanted to gain the cultural upper hand by defining themselves against each other. But the official world has also had a major role to play. The story as it is frequently told begins with the use of Ecstasy in the context of all-night dancing to 'house' music in huge fantasy discotheques on the Balearic island of Ibiza. The combination of mid-eighties Yuppie, hippy carefreeness (Ibiza was invaded by hippies in the sixties) and holiday hedonism forged a 'Balearic' lifestyle or 'vibe' here which became very influential. Back in London, a number of clubbers attempted to 'relive the dream' and 'Acid House', along with its psychedelia and peace and love, emerged. But this story is only one of many. It overlooks the key role played by black and gay club cultures in Chicago, New York and Detroit. It's a particularly southern story too. Up in the North of England, it meant little to the ex-soccer Casuals, working class and fiercely dismissive of everything 'London' and hippyish, who were key in defining the 'Madchester' style in music, clothes, haircuts, cultural entrepreneurialism and drugtaking, with the Hacienda nightclub and Factory Records at its core. Never mind over the border in 'Trainspotting' Scotland.

Told by the media, the story is different again. Not inappropriately, it was the youth style magazine of the eighties, *The Face*, which first heralded Ecstasy's coming to the nation's youth:

> As the trappings of the psychedelic era resurface in clothes and music, the
> real force behind those times is left untapped: the desire for a transformation
> of consciousness. But there is a drug whose advocates claim it will do
> just that.
>
> (NASMYTH, 1985)

The article was reporting on America's 'Drug of the Eighties', a drug which promised to fulfil a longing for innocent euphoria, made you feel very close and empathetic but not rapturous like the name suggested, was 'everywhere' in America and had been made illegal earlier in the year. Up until then, Ecstasy was available over the US counter in clubs, chargeable to all major credit cards and came with

IT TAKES TWO (GENERATIONS) TO TANGO

'flight instructions'. You may not have been able to read the book or see the film but the T-shirt and bumper sticker were definitely available, warning: 'Don't get married for six weeks after XTC'. Although it reported that the drug was known to only a few in Britain in the fashion, media and music industries, the article left little doubt of its presence on this side of the Atlantic. Thus was curiosity in the drug aroused among a key audience – an article by the same author a year later noted that use of Ecstasy had increased tenfold during that time (Nasmyth, 1986).

In the autumn of 1988 'Acid House', went overground, cast as an 'evil' and 'warped' drug cult into which the nation's young were being enticed by sinister 'Mr Bigs' and drug dealers. Pictures of thousands of seemingly drug-crazed youngsters, combined with the first death associated with Ecstasy, added to the list of adult social anxiety enough to create the feeling that something needed to be done. A media hungry for the sex, shock and seediness which was part of its staple diet, together with a government well ensconced in an American-style drugs and crime war made sure of it.

And so the relationship between the mainstream, official 'adult' worlds and the 'underground' worlds of youth, which has been crucial to this cultural transformation's process developed. The official world responded to the nuisance value and potentially subversive nature of large numbers of young people from different backgrounds, cultures and parts of the country gathering together to dance to 'house' music under the influence of stimulant and psychedelic drugs with surveillance and legislation. Its effect was opposite to the desired one. Instead of curbing the phenomenon, the Licensing Act, 1988, the Entertainments (Increased Penalties Act), 1990 and specialist police units, simply changed the nascent culture's scale and structure. Devotees who viewed themselves as 'authentic' in contrast to the 'Acid Teds' (or mainstream youth) who had jumped on the 'Acid House' bandwagon along with Top Shop and The Sun, dropped 'Acid

House' culture (the particular form of 'house' music, the dancing style and the clothes – but *not* the drugs) in favour of something far less mainstream. An article entitled, 'Who Killed Smiley?', makes this clear:

> *Don't look for a Smiley or the word 'acid' if you're after the real underground clubs, they've left all that to the copyists … Whatever you do don't check the press for details. The summer of love goes on – underground.*
> (OFFBEAT, 1988)

In the legal clubs and more illicit venues, mainstream and underground, the weekend way of young hedonistic life thrived. 'Rave' became big business, not only of the dodgy criminal kind, but also making a huge impact on popular youth culture – from nightclubs and fashion retail outlets, to youth TV, style magazines and even the football terraces. By 1992, even magazines for young teenagers bore the signs of its popularity. While obviously eager to avoid appearing to condone drug use in any way, *Smash Hits* magazine advertised '8 pages of Rave stuff inside' on its October 1992 cover. Entitled 'Get Sorted', this piece employed the language associated with a now mainstream popular youth culture. Language with drug connotations obvious to those 'in the know'. By January 1993, it was evident that even that tired stalwart of popular culture, the Christmas panto, had to acknowledge the phenomenon. The second *Sunday Mirror* of the year reported that: 'Cinderella panto bosses shouted "Oh no you don't!" when the fairy Godmother told an Ugly Sister: "Let's fly to heaven on a cloud of ecstasy!". "It sounded like Cinderella was going to a rave rather than a ball", said one of the cast in Cleckheaton, W. Yorks. The line was changed to: "Let's fly to heaven on a cloud".' (*Sunday Mirror*, 1993).

And so the process has continued. The official world has simultaneously pictured a generation of youth enslaved to 'killer

IT TAKES TWO (GENERATIONS) TO TANGO

music' and drugs which, if they don't kill, cause psychological damage; while showing no qualms when there was money to be made by picking up on this youthworld and selling it to a wider audience. Meanwhile the music, dress styles and general cultures of young people have continued to diversify – those with an eye to mainstream avoidance have kept up the game of mainstream/underground tag. So have their drugtaking habits as alcohol, more powerful psychedelic drugs, barbiturates, cocaine and rock cocaine have made their way into the wide range of venues, inside and outside, playing ever-changing varieties of 'House' and associated style music.

It is coming up to two years since the official world launched a massive attack on the culture. The Criminal Justice and Public Order Act of October 1994 introduced a variety of legal rulings and powers for the police which affect people who go to dance clubs and parties: Section 47 of the Act made it an offence to make preparations to hold, wait for or attend a rave;[1] Section 45 gave the police powers to arrest, without a warrant, trespassers failing to leave the site of a rave after being asked to do so by a police officer; Section 49 gave the police powers to control traffic within a five mile radius of a rave, including the authority to stop vehicles at a roadblock. But, although it may have significantly changed the shape of the end-of-the-century youth party, this major attempt to 'poop' it hasn't succeeded. The party goes on. Each time the parents say Just Say No, it seems to make more young folk say yes.

Interestingly, dancing in Britain after dark has been the most popular form of entertainment since the Tory government first took office. Admissions to sporting events, cinemas and all the 'live arts' combined were substantially lower than those to dance events between 1979 and 1994 (Leisure Consultants, 1990). But all of this, until recently, passed most of the adult world by. The media death of Leah Betts after taking Ecstasy at her 18th birthday party (although one of at least fifty reported over the decade) finally opened the adult population's eyes to a cultural phenomenon which they still don't understand but in which, they now know, the use of the now infamous drug Ecstasy has played an important, but by no means exclusive, role:

> We walk now in a veiled land, adjoined to and yet separate from the country in which we grew up and left other generations behind. In this over-the-rainbow leisure land, the symbols and signs of the culture born of the Ecstasy-driven rave are a universal language, as comprehensible to the working class boy in Paisley as to the public schoolgirl in Surrey. And yet even now, on the other side of the veil, those things ... are everywhere but meaningless. It is as if there is an invisible world existing within the official one ... The problem for those in the official world is that to see through a veil properly, you cannot merely shine a light at it from where you are. You must have illumination from the other side. The first beam of light penetrated in November 1995 ... because Leah Betts proved how linked the veiled and unveiled worlds were: on the night she took Ecstasy ... she was sitting in her mum and dad's living room having a birthday party while they sat in the kitchen. When the veil was lifted, it was found that the veiled and unveiled worlds were not merely close to one another. They were the same.
>
> THE FACE (BENSON, 1996)

1 A rave is described in the Act as 'a gathering of a hundred or more persons, whether or not trespassers, at which amplified music is played during the night'. The relevant type of music is described as 'that which is wholly or predominantly characterised by the emission of a succession of repetitive beats'.

IT TAKES TWO (GENERATIONS) TO TANGO

PART 2

The Case

The case so far

I started writing this book early in 1996, at a time when Ecstasy
fever was running high in the British public mind following a spate of
Ecstasy-related deaths (particularly that of Leah Betts the previous
November). However, as the weeks went by, the Ecstasy media saga
reached another 'stop' in its seemingly endless 'stop'/'go' cycle. How
long this relative lull will last is anyone's guess but you can bet your
life there will be another 'go' phase. The Ecstasy case is opened in the
British public arena, then it is shut. But it is never solved, even though
everyone except, perhaps, the nation's youth, wants to solve it. The
young carry on partying and the adult population carries on
concerning itself with how to pull the plug. One side of the generation
divide seems bent on a quick fix of happiness, euphoria, a feeling of
belonging. The other side seems driven to find a quick fix to solve
what they see as a huge problem. As I said before, a major motor to
the cultural phenomenon of which the drug Ecstasy has become
symbolic has been the cultural divide between the young and the

not-so-young, between a world-within-a-world and the official world. I have re-opened the 'E' files to pursue that line of inquiry but, before I do, I will run over the case so far, as I see it.

Picture, if you will, a TV debate which covers the important issues of the day with a presenter and an invited studio audience. Be it 'serious' or more voxpop, the TV debate has been one of the only public places where a broad range of the players in the Ecstasy case have actually (ostensibly at least) met and talked to one another. It is also a handy way of picturing the overall state of play.

First, who are the people taking part? The general routine is that invited 'experts' of various kinds are brought into the discussion at key moments by the presenter, then the broader mass of 'common people' get to have their say. You can always bank on there being at least one medical expert of some kind – someone who knows about the medical 'facts' relating to Ecstasy and, maybe, other drugs. Recently, as Ecstasy-related death has risen on the agenda, pathologists have gained more air time. There is almost always at least one politician, often a government spokesperson, and often a policeman too. Non-medical drug 'experts' (either in care services, drug education or research) usually get wheeled on as well. Sometimes, there's a representative of 'young people' or, usually, someone who will admit to having used Ecstasy. There is also at least one parent deeply affected by their child's Ecstasy use.

What frequently happens in these debates is that the presenter attempts to 'get to the bottom of it all' in some way: 'Ecstasy, a harmless bit of youthful fun or a nightmare?' 'Ecstasy or agony?' The quest always appears to be to solve the Ecstasy case but in fact what happens is that the same arguments are rerun. A cultural phenomenon is shrunk to handy debating size – revolving around the use of a drug and the nature of risk. The medical experts and politicians slog it out, trading scientific facts for the moral high ground. The policemen, more often than not, express the grave difficulties they have in policing drugs. The non-medical experts attempt to inject some rationality in vain. The experiential 'experts', the parents and the Ecstasy users, get caught up in their own emotion. Everyday folk, between them, echo all of these views. Result? Stalemate. Prohibition? Legalisation? We've seen it all before. All the players go home and carry on in their own sweet (or not so sweet) way.

A similar thing happens in the public arena as a whole – most of the players profess to want a solution to the Ecstasy case. Certainty is the name of the game. Most focus narrowly on the nature of the drug. They shout out their solutions across the public arena, instead of a TV studio. But while in the TV studio, the players shouting the loudest are often those trying to make themselves heard because they don't get heard elsewhere – everyday folk from both Planets Youth and Middle Age. In the public arena the politicians, the professional experts and the media itself drown them out almost entirely. The public Ecstasy case is largely a conversation between adults in the official world. They are the ones who feel they must, at least, be seen to take responsibility and do something.

The grown-up official world quick fix is based on certainty of two main kinds: one governing, one in opposition. Both look to the law and its enforcement, as well as education for a solution. The governing position is based on the certainty that 'it's great when you're straight' (even if you get pissed, smoke tobacco and go to the doctor for a sleeping tablet or tranquilliser). From this position, Ecstasy is guilty of not only corrupting but also killing and maiming the young by enticing them with the false promise of pleasure. The drug sucks the youthful innocent into a world of crime and danger, where they will get 'hooked' on other drugs – their bodies, minds and morals shot to smithereens. And not only they, but their families and communities suffer. At this pole, the Ecstasy case is fundamentally a moral one – all drugs are bad. This camp on the moral high ground houses the majority of politicians and much of the media. The more liberal wing acknowledges the harms of alcohol and tobacco but argues that, if we had known what we now know about these drugs, they would also never have been licensed. This prohibition camp deals so heavily in certainty that it frames all public debate. Anyone who doesn't agree is forced into a position of equal certainty. If you don't condemn, then you condone. If you don't think stopping drugs is achievable, then you automatically think drugs are good. End of story.

The adult opposition, meanwhile, counter-attacks by attempting to occupy a moral-free zone. Forget whether drugs are good or bad, this case rests on the certainty that we need to get rational and practical, to 'Get Real'. There are a number of camps on this seemingly moral low ground but they all consider that: drugs are here to stay – too many people have just said yes to illicit drugs and the illegal supply industry is too entrenched; some drugs carry more risk than others; and it's hypocritical to single out only alcohol and tobacco for legitimate production/distribution, state sponsorship and social control. The camps run from the libertarians (see, for instance, some young Tories, the odd right-wing judge, the drugs charity Release, Lord Mancroft, Chair of the Drug and Alcohol charity), who come out and say we should legalise drugs, through to more guarded but forthright calls to 'decriminalise' (like the Secretary-General of Interpol) to a much more mealy-mouthed, 'let's re-examine the drug licensing framework and policing of drugs' approach (some senior policemen and senior players in youthwork, the Liberal Democratic Party, as well as a lot of workers in the drug policy and service field).

THE OFFICIAL MORAL HIGH GROUND

Out on the moral high ground the Ecstasy quick fix is morally justified and simple – stop the supply of drugs through law enforcement, bang up all the dealers and the persistent users and educate the young folk to Just Say No. Illegal drug use of any kind is a threat to the very social fabric. Bravely going where no man has gone before on the drugs front and achieving a drug-free society (except state-sponsored ones) is a fraught but achievable goal.

The drugs epidemic is a scourge as terrible as any medieval plague. Let us, as a nation, make a New Year resolution that 1996 is the year in which we will turn the tide of drug abuse which is threatening our civilisation. Our aim is nothing less than to win back Scotland from the drug culture and liberate a generation.

Michael Forsyth, the Secretary of State for Scotland, gave this New Year message at the launch of the 1996 Scotland Against Drugs campaign which speaks loud and clear the governing position on drugs with which we're so familiar. The British Government and, particularly, the tabloid press have waged a War On Drugs, with little gripe from the Opposition. Heroin, crack, Ecstasy, you name it, they've all been getting the same mortal combat treatment since the mid-eighties.

Tabloid campaigns against Ecstasy have been endorsed by the government. In *The Daily Star* in 1992, under a headline, 'Getting tough on evil Ecstasy', Home Office Minister John Patten was quoted as saying, 'The Star's campaign is a good preventative one. Reaching people in simple language is very important' about a campaign which portrayed Ecstasy as 'The enemy of our kids'. In a similar vein, the government's hard-hitting anti-drugs approach, all shock tactics and no real information, told us 'Heroin Screws You Up' in 1985/6, 'Smack

Isn't Worth It' in 1987, 'Drugs: The Effects Can Last Forever' and 'You Can Only Come Down' in 1990, through the mass media. Kids in the classroom have been told in any number of ways to, à la Nancy Reagan, Just Say No. Ex-junkies have been dragged in to show them how bad it can get, along with, perhaps, a kindly bobby on the beat.

But the young have kept on saying yes and, as it has got harder for the government to ignore the fact that rather more young folk seem to be taking drugs other than the drug classics (like heroin and solvents) and the new demons (like crack) than ever before – with studies increasingly showing at least half of teenagers having tried an illicit drug – so the messages have become more mixed.

> Drug misuse among young people is not just a problem in inner cities – it occurs in leafy suburbs and rural areas as well. It extends across social and economic boundaries and different communities ... We need to equip young people with the facts to enable them to make healthy, informed decisions and the skills to resist peer and other pressures. But in doing that we must be aware of the need to make our messages to young people credible.
> THE RT HON TONY NEWTON (THEN LEADER OF THE HOUSE OF COMMONS), AT A
> CONFERENCE, 'YOUTH CULTURE-DRUGS CULTURE?', AT THE GUILDHALL,
> LONDON, 1994.

The government's three-year National Drugs Strategy (for England), 'Tackling Drugs Together', unveiled in a White Paper in May 1995, stressed its emphasis on law enforcement and reducing the supply of drugs but it also struck rather a different tone. As part of its recognition of the need for 'stronger action on reducing the demand for drugs', it acknowledged that shock horror tactics were not the most effective approach. There were no drug demons, no hellfire, just enabling, healthy decisions based on fact and skills development. While standing firm on the stopping drugs front, the strategy also had a 'get real' element reminiscent of the drug debate opposition: a secondary goal of 'harm minimisation' was accepted (at least where all else fails). The White Paper, for instance, recommended that 'suitable health and safety measures' such as cold drinking water, should be made available at clubs 'irrespective of whether drugs are being taken' – by owners or organisers. And part of the Health Education Authority's three-year drugs and solvents publicity campaign (launched in November 1995 with the National Drugs Helpline) has seen the distribution of postcards giving information on water and Ecstasy and how to cope if someone has a bad trip on LSD being distributed in clubs, shops and cafés. Suddenly Tony Newton has had to discuss 'the fine line' between being seen to condone and to condemn drugs. Does all this talk of giving people the facts to make up their own minds mean the government has gone soft on drugs?

Hardly. The British government is still firing on all moral cylinders when it comes to the drugs question. What is more, its version of 'giving people the facts' (an idea that has been around since the seventies) is based on the assumption that having information is enough to stop you doing something. Now 'Just Say No' is purely a matter of informed decision. Take the current (American-inspired) measures, endorsed by the Department of Education under the rubric of 'Tackling Drugs Together' in a series of regional conferences in early 1996 which formed part of an initiative called 'Drug Proof': Drug Abuse Resistance Education (DARE) programmes and Rotary Club-assisted Life Education Centres. These measures favour factual information about drugs but also emphasise: values which assume that people with a sense of personal responsibility will not take drugs; refusal skills which assume young people are prey to peer pressure and only need to develop the skills to Just Say No; decision-making skills so rational choices to not take drugs can be made; boosting self-esteem as a guard against the need to take drugs; and offering alternative highs (particularly sports), as a replacement for the excitement of taking drugs (Cohen, 1996).

And what's so wrong with that?

MORAL-FREE AND PRACTICAL: THE OPPOSITION

Out in the moral-free zone of the opposition, the answer is, 'Quite a lot'. Stopping people from taking drugs is a fool's dream, they say. Just look at the decades of shock horror and more recent factual anti-smoking campaigns. While the population as a whole may be smoking less, more young people seem to be smoking earlier than they ever have. You only have to look at the case of 'Death' cigarettes to see just how useless threatening the young with death really is. A special brand sold in a black packet with a skull, 'Death' sold by the shedload. Knowing about tar-blackened lungs and cancer deaths doesn't stop cigarette sales. In a similar way, the rationalists argue, being scared by images of death and destruction, or knowing about the potential risk of liver or brain damage, etc doesn't stop the use of other, currently illegal drugs. Look at all the evaluations of drugs education from the seventies to the present day, they cry.

In Britain and all over the world, there is no well-supported evidence that drugs education gets young people to stay away from drugs or stops them when they've started. Research suggests that the DARE programmes becoming popular in this country are ineffective and, if anything, encourage young people to scapegoat drug users as weak and/or evil (Ennett et al, 1994) and Life Education Centres appear, if anything, more likely to result in more young people using drugs. Some evaluations have found that scare tactics may even glamorise drugs (Hawthorne et al, 1995). Meanwhile, taking drugs has always been a fundamental part of the human condition, the rationalists assert. Look at the ancient civilisations and the latter-day tribes who have done everything from psychedelic toads to the good old-fashioned opium poppy. And if you think you can control this human activity, police it out of existence, just look at the nation's prisons. The most controlled environment you can possibly get and it's awash with drugs.

The answer for many in the let's-calm-down-and-get-sensible camp, as I said before, is to change the legal status or policing of some or all drugs. Alter the legal status of currently illegal drugs, some argue, and quality control could be introduced, a basic human right to choose to use mind-changing substances would be honoured, *and* the Treasury's coffers would be filled. At the very least, follow the ultra-rationalist example of the Dutch approach as a baseline and take the crime out of obtaining and consuming cannabis by changing the way its distribution is policed. The same arguments have been applied to Ecstasy. Control its quality and you'll control much of the harm increasingly associated with the drug. Although not necessarily linked to calls for changing the law or policing of drugs, calls for the introduction of testing tablets at nightclubs and other dance venues prior to use are also based on the Dutch rational approach and example. But, although the moral-free zoners see their calls as calls for calm and commonsense, themselves a reply to the moral razzamatazz of the other side, the governing moral force sees (or says it sees) only one thing – the moral-free zoners advocate the use of drugs. Of course, this makes for even more demands for commonsense and calm and ... so the cycle goes on.

JUST SAY KNOW ... QUICK FIX-FREE AS WELL AS MORAL-FREE

It's at this point of non-solution that we find a different brand of 'getting practical and sensible' in the Ecstasy case being pursued in the official world. It, like the ruling prohibitionists and opposing legalisers/decriminalisers, has been part of the wider drugs case for some time. Just not quite so long. It went public in a big way when the HIV virus was found among injecting drug users in the eighties and fear that this might spell AIDS for the population at large was running high in Britain. Called 'harm reduction' or 'harm minimisation', this position shares with the opposition in the drugs debate a basic acceptance that drugs aren't going away and that a lot of people who have said yes to them aren't necessarily going to give up. But in this camp, they want to leave the prohibition/legalisation vicious cycle well behind and get *really* practical and sensible.

From this position, there is no big solution to the Ecstasy, or any other drug case. Just more or less effective ways of dealing with it. The best we can do is to give up 'telling lies' or giving the young information which in no way matches their experience ('they're telling me drugs are bad but they make me feel so good') and develop ways of giving people the best information available about drugs – giving the good as well as bad effects, their legal status etc. We should additionally take any other measures we can to reduce the harms (to the body, the mind, the purse, the (non-)criminal record, other people) drugs may cause. This camp was there waiting when the government needed to do something about HIV and AIDS among injecting drug users. Result? A U-turn on the governmental moral crusade against drugs in the late eighties, in one area of policy anyway – the introduction of needle exchanges, information campaigns and what was called 'flexible prescribing' of heroin substitute, methadone, to change the behaviour of drug users sharing injecting equipment. And because many of its proponents tend to be closer to drug worlds than most in the official world (not only because they take 'drugology' – my word not theirs – seriously but also because they see keeping in touch with drug cultures as a key part of their job), it was this camp which first alerted the social policy world to the coming of Ecstasy and the new drug ethic which went with it.

'Chill Out' – A Raver's Guide, a leaflet produced by a drug information agency in Liverpool (then called 'Mersey Drug Training and Information Centre' or 'MDTIC', now 'HIT') was a prime example of both the approach and the response it can receive. Funded by the then Mersey Regional Health Authority in September 1991, it was a response to a growing number of calls to the agency and insider contact with the growing culturE. Three categories of potential harm related to Ecstasy and other 'dance drug' use had been identified by the leaflet's producers – drug specific, situational and social – and it contained basic information about the three main drugs then used on the club scene – Ecstasy, LSD and amphetamine. Resembling the flyers used to advertise events and club nights, it was distributed through specialist clothes and record shops, through advertisements in magazines, on radio and in bars, cafés and clubs. An input was also made into 'hip' magazine The Face which created a great deal of reader response (McDermott et al, 1992).

Although it went down well on Planet Youth, the leaflet was blasted in the tabloid press, first local (Liverpool Echo, 1992) and then national (Daily Star, 1992; The Sun, 1992). 'Raving Mad' the Liverpool Echo kicked off. 'Fury At Sex Guide To 'E'" said the front page of The Sun next day. 'What a Dope!' The Daily Star's front page added on the same day, in a more personalised attack on the director of MDTIC. But although there were great shenanigans as the horror of these 'loony leaflets' got talked up to fever pitch in a Britain facing an election, a government award for Ecstasy research (confirmed only that morning) was withdrawn from MDTIC and the leaflet was amended, the old adage that bad publicity is better than no publicity proved more than true. The controversy was somewhat short-lived but sales of the leaflet boomed and support for the campaign was voiced in Liverpool's sister newspaper, the Daily Post, in the Manchester Evening News, by the general public in Liverpool (via letters to the Liverpool Echo), and by a number of drug and health agencies.

The 'harm reductionist' position in the Ecstasy case has been Just Say Know and the 'Chill Out' example suggests that it does have supporters among ordinary folk, on both sides of the generational divide. Sales of harm reduction materials to schools and youth services have mushroomed, as the government has adjusted its drugs war-speak a little by taking on some 'harm reductionist' words (Cohen, 1996). This brand of harm reduction has also been about credibility with the target audience – or 'source credibility' as the health educationalists call it. Both 'Chill Out' and a series of cartoon-style leaflets involving a character called 'Peanut Pete', the archetypal white working-class lad in the jobless nineties, produced by the Lifeline Project in Manchester, traded, in different ways, on demonstrating that their producers knew a great deal about all the (changing) components of 'dance drug' culture – from clothes styles to the codes of behaviour appropriate to different settings, to 'in' phrases and idioms – the whole ethic. Proof that this kind of drugs education works is thinner on the ground than attempts to prove the Just Say No case. However, a recent British review of evaluation studies of drugs education of all kinds concluded that drugs education doesn't stop people taking drugs and the best we can hope for is to limit people who've already tried drugs from overdoing it or to reduce drug-related harm (Dorn and Murji, 1992).

CERTAINTY AND SCIENCE: ENOUGH FOR ORDINARY FOLK?

So there you have it. The lie of the official land in the Ecstasy case so far. The professionals who slog it out in the official world. The trade in solutions where certainty is the currency. But how certain is certain? And where do ordinary people on Planets Youth and Middle Age fit in? While the professionals in the official world try to fix things, the common folk have to live with it, try and make sense of it all.

First Just Say Think about how certain the world that trades in certainties really is. I put it to you that, ultimately, the answer is not very. I know what it is like to be drawn into certainty. Most of my research over the past seven years has been ultimately tied up with the question of prevention and policymaking around drugs in one way or another. It is part of my job to deal in certainty, to draw conclusions on which to base policy; to take a position in conference debates and media interviews. Everyone wants certainty. The parents, teachers, youth and community workers I interview want it, for sure. But look at the case for preventing use of Ecstasy and other drugs through education, for instance. Proving beyond doubt that kids either haven't started taking drugs or have stopped because of short, sharp shocks or information they've received is tricky for the Just Say No supporters. Especially given the fact that we have little on-going large-scale information on the nation's drug-taking habits and that so many evaluations don't even try to assess the information campaign's target audience's drug-taking habits before and after the event. Similarly, proving that information has made a positive impact on drug-related harms is equally tricky. Giving someone credible and accurate information about drugs is one thing. Proving they do or don't do something now (like mix drugs, take too many at once, dance too long without rests, etc) which they did before getting the information is quite another. Perhaps the most public demonstration of the approach's effectiveness on the Ecstasy front came when coverage of the death of Leah Betts and others – where drinking too much water appeared to be involved – seemed to demonstrate that one of the key harm reduction messages had got through with disastrous effect. One of the key messages of campaigns had been to avoid heatstroke by drinking (non-alcoholic) liquid. Based on a careful appraisal of all the research then available, this seemed a highly appropriate message if your aim was to reduce the amount of harm someone using Ecstasy in a hot nightclub may come to. But this proof has been a mixed blessing – it made the Just Say Know supporters sitting ducks for potshots from the moral high grounders.

Look also at the role of that ultimate certainty, science, in the case. Knowing more about drugs is surely the sensible and reasonable person's solution to the problem. It is not a question of good or bad, it is just ... fact. How does Ecstasy really kill? What are its long-term effects on the mind and body? These are surely the hundred dollar questions? And there are medical experts to answer them (although research on Ecstasy is still relatively thin on the ground). But is definitive proof that Ecstasy really does/does not kill, is/is not toxic, does/does not cause brain damage, etc an achievable goal? For one thing, medical research on street drugs is notoriously difficult – their content and quality vary so widely, the 'laboratory' conditions of a controlled study are difficult, if not impossible to achieve. The environment in nightclubs, urban wastelands and fields, the most common places of Ecstasy use, would also be difficult to reproduce and control. For another thing, one person's definitive proof is another's inconclusive study. Facts have a nasty way of carrying both question marks and comforters, depending on your faith.

Ultimately, much of the certainty which has been expressed in the Ecstasy (and other drugs) case is based on faith and conviction, not science. The Just Say No supporters act on their conviction that drugs are wrong and should be got rid of. And their faith shows in their moral-speak. They are unperturbed by their lack of 'success' (ie people still take drugs and more people are doing it) and carry on doing what they do best – addressing the fears of the adult world. The Just Say Know supporters are equally strong in their conviction that drugs are here to stay. But they are less up front about their morals than those proclaimed by the opposing side. Behind the let's-get-practical approach, there is a set of values, world views which are different from those of the other side – not just on drugs, but sex, relationships, families, you name it.

That's not to say the Just Say Knowers are all crazed druggies on the side, like the ruling morality would have us believe. Rather than 'drugs are good', the view they subscribe to is more 'not all altered states of mind are bad but hypocrisy is.' They ultimately define their 'success' in terms of the popularity of their work among their target audience – in the Ecstasy case, the young. People whose values and world views may be closer to their own.

So, in the Ecstasy case, we have an official world where professionals from opposing sides talk at each other in the name of others, the ordinary folk of all ages. The pressure is on them to offer solutions and offer them they do – although these are based mostly on faith or conviction rather than science at the end of the day. But this cycle of razzamatazz leaves the constituencies whose flesh they press in a state. One half of the equation – much of the adult population and a lot of under 14s – has everyday worries regularly stimulated by the moral high grounders. They try to keep the certainty alive but also live in fear of something they know little about. The other half mostly like it to be this way and respond accordingly – with a different kind of certainty, the certainty of Ease. Looking at the relationship between this popular fear and ease is how I mean to develop my new line of inquiry in the Ecstasy case – to show you just how unsolved it really it is.

3

Fear, ease and beyond

SUCH A BAD FEELING

If there is one headline which has dominated the media Ecstasy saga it's 'The Agony and the Ecstasy'. When I read it now, all I can think of are authors and sub-editors, too bored and tired to give of their best. Actually it's a telling phrase. Apart from giving the whole thing a quasi-religious feel, it illustrates a huge generational divide in the Ecstasy case. On the one hand fEar, on the other Ease – the one feeding the other in an endless cycle of emotion. The louder an official world damns the cultural (pre-) occupation of the younger generation in moralistic terms and the more afraid the adult world becomes, the more ease has been required on Planet Youth. The more the young's apparent ease is identified, the bigger fear becomes. One side seeks quick-fix solutions, the other just wants a quick fix. And so it goes on. You only have to look at the current number one public concern about Ecstasy to see how this works.

FEAR

The fashion for Ecstasy must die like our daughter died.
MRS JANET BETTS AT THE PRESS CONFERENCE FOLLOWING HER STEP-DAUGHTER
LEAH'S DEATH

In Britain in early 1996, the adult population's fears of and for a
generation seemingly devoted to altered states of mind are publicly
voiced as one – death. The nation's parents are afraid their children
will take a pill and die. The drugs melodrama is high on their worry
list and its leading character, cast by the moral high grounders, is the
innocent victim – the single white female. Her face at the time of
writing this book was that of the young Essex girl who died after
taking Ecstasy at her 18th birthday party. Although her funeral has
taken place and been filmed and circulated as a warning to other
young people, Leah Betts has far from been laid to rest. Her happy
smiling face on the one hand and, on the other, lying in a coma with
life-support tubes and pipes, is still very much a part of the fabric of
everyday English life in early 1996. Ask anyone in Britain about the
drug Ecstasy and the chances are they'll mention her name (just like
all the people I interviewed following her death until summer 1996 –
young or old).

The tragedy of this pretty white Essex teenager's death after
taking Ecstasy at her 18th birthday party continues to frame public
perception of drugs in Britain. The blow-by-blow press coverage of
Leah Betts' collapse, death and funeral (encouraged by her parents'
desire to use her tragic example to deter other young people from a
similar fate) set the iconography of fEar in stone. 'Bags of death' said
Paul Betts, her father, when, in one of his many ensuing television
appearances, confronted with large bags of Ecstasy seized by the
authorities. For many among the generations on the other side of the
Ecstasy hill, who only ever hear about the drug Ecstasy when

something goes wrong, British youth is under threat – from a drug which, while promising pleasure, can and does actually kill. Forget all the other fears over the years since 1988 for now, more than ever before, Ecstasy = death. Plain and simple.

The latest wave of fear began in October 1996 when 17-year-old Daniel Ashton died after taking a tablet in a Blackpool nightclub. A week later, two young men were on trial in Buckinghamshire, accused of supplying Ecstasy in September 1994 to a sixth-former who had subsequently died (they were acquitted). The 'Evils of Ecstasy' were re-run in the tabloids, as old stories were raked over – like that of Clare Leighton, who died in 1989 from a rare allergic reaction to the drug. Within a month, the Betts' misfortune became their real scoop. 1996 began much as it had ended with the drugs saga very much in the headlines. The nervy tone struck by the pre-Christmas tragedy of the Betts family and the campaigns that followed, was sustained by the reported experience of another East Anglian family. This next Ecstasy episode, however, involved a happier ending if the same salutary message. Nineteen-year-old Helen Cousins collapsed and went into a coma after leaving a club in Peterborough on New Year's Day but she happily lived to tell the press that 'Ecstasy isn't worth the dance with death'. Read out by her relieved mother because Helen was still unable to speak following a tracheotomy performed while she was in intensive care, this message was significant. Here was a young woman lucky enough to return from the jaws of death, a young victim who lived to tell the tale like the adult world wanted to hear it. Soon after, 19-year-old Andreas Bouzis was not so fortunate. He collapsed after taking the drug at a club in South London and died. A year on from when adverts for the new National Lottery first told the nation 'It could be you', the adult population were terrified that their kids were buying into a deadly Ecstasy lottery. 'It Could Be Your Child' warned the *Daily Mail* in November 1995. 'Who'll Be The Next?' asked the *Eastern Daily Press* in January 1996.

DANCING WITH A COCKTAIL OF DEATH: PUTTING THE 'E' IN FEAR

The Acid House craze now sweeping discos is putting thousands of teenagers in peril. One girl has died after taking the mind-bending Ecstasy ... But what can be done to stop this crazy cult? ... It isn't smart. It isn't clever. It's just deadly. As 21-year-old Janet Mayes found out ... THE HARDEST WAY OF ALL.

DAILY STAR 1988

By 1996, there was quite a history to this version of adult fear. A key medium we can turn to to illustrate it best is the tabloid press. Much maligned and now part of a wide range of national and international media, it nonetheless has played a key role in determining the volume and shape of fear in the Ecstasy case.

For one thing, it still provides over half the British population with their daily reading. For another, it has religiously picked up on Ecstasy-related mishaps and publicized them freely, playing a role in the stop/go Ecstasy media saga. For yet another, the tabloids' predictable response to that early manifestation of culturE in 1988, 'Acid House', was actively courted by a canny section of the British music press. A response which was to pressure the official world to act (and in so doing, to cause culturE to multiply). In February 1988, the three then main music weeklies ran stories about acid house, pondering 'how long it will be before our moral guardians start claiming that promoting the music is helping to promote drug-taking among the young?' (*Record Mirror*, February 20, 1988). During that summer, they wrote about Ecstasy use in the clubs and by the end of August were wondering why the tabloids were ignoring the issue. Ecstasy had 'received little of the gutter press scare treatment afforded Crack yet the drug has yet to make any real inroads into British drug culture' (*New Musical Express*, 13 August, 1988). But, said

Time Out, 'It's not hard to imagine the angle the tabloid press will choose if they "report" on the acid house scene' (17–24 August 1988). All this 'talking up' finally paid off in the autumn (Thornton, 1995).

And almost immediately, the single white female took up her leading role in the 'stop-go' media Ecstasy drama. *The Daily Star*'s 'dancing with a cocktail of death' feature was one of many which reported that Britain was flooded with 'kill pills' in the autumn of 1988, following the collapse at an Acid House disco in Surrey and subsequent death of 21-year-old Essex girl Janet Mayes, a children's nanny, in October (*Daily Star*, 1988). 'The drug pushers that killed my daughter should be shot', her distraught mother was reported as saying, in a now-familiar scenario of blame (*Daily Express*, 1988). For a brief period she became a reference point, a quote factor for drug stories, just like Leah Betts' parents seven years later. Unlike them, her media career was short-lived.

Although it had never previously taken on the public significance it achieved in Britain as 1995 ended and 1996 began, the equation between Ecstasy and death has been drummed into the British public perennially ever since:

The Sun 'Girl 21 Drops Dead At Acid Disco' (October 19, 1988)

Manchester Evening News 'Tragedy Of Acid House Drug Girl' (July 16, 1989)

The Sun 'Tragic Ecstasy Lad Was On His First trip (May 14, 1991)

Daily Star 'Nightmare Of Super E. It's Deadlier Than Ever And On Sale For £12' (October 13, 1992)

Manchester Evening News 'Ecstasy Kills Club Boy 15' (February 21, 1994)

Tabloid reporting of these tragic deaths has tended to follow a formula. The innocence of each unfortunate young person concerned, so vital to the bigger moral picture, is established with some key ingredients, milked to the maximum. 1) They only tried Ecstasy once, 2) they were just a normal young person, 3) they took the pill unknowingly, or (failing this) 4) they were forced to take the pill by an evil pusher or deranged peers, 5) they had everything to live for, 6) their (distressed) parent(s) (usually mother) is/are interviewed, photographed and consulted as experts in ensuing coverage. While by no means wishing to add to the pain and sorrow of the relatives and friends of those young people concerned, I have to say that this reporting has, in its myth creation, been somewhat inaccurate. The Leah Betts case is one in point. First, we were told, she'd taken her first Ecstasy tablet on that fateful night, then it transpired she had taken Ecstasy previously and tried other drugs too.

Of course, the drugs melodrama is not simply a tabloid saga conjured from thin air. It fits hand in glove with the official moral high ground image of Ecstasy use. And, more to the point, real personal tragedy guides the script. It is only possible to nurture this fear in the adult population as a whole, especially parents, because it touches a raw nerve – the deep dark fear of losing a child:

> One Friday Andreas went to a club just as your child may have done. Now he is dead. He is gone forever. I cannot describe our feelings, everything we have had over the last 19 years has been taken away.
> MRS JOSEPHINE BOUZIS AT A PRESS CONFERENCE FOLLOWING HER SON'S DEATH.

> Don't chance your life. It can happen to you if you take Ecstasy. It can take your life. Nothing is worth that. Don't weaken. Be strong. Say no.
> MRS COUSINS AT A PRESS CONFERENCE AFTER HER DAUGHTER HAD RECOVERED FROM A COMA.

Any parent hearing Mrs Bouzis' words would experience heartfelt sympathy and fear. The very thought of losing your child to an untimely death is unbearable, looking such a possibility in the eye is … well indescribable. And any parent would follow Mrs Cousins' logic, reach the same conclusion. Viewed from this perspective, Ecstasy just is not and can never be worth such a risk.

EASE

PARTY HAPPENING PEOPLE: YOU NEVER HAD IT SO GOOD

While the adult population is mortally afraid of a pill which can kill the young, the young are embracing the cultures in which this pill has played a formative part. Take a look at another face, another character playing on a different stage to a different audience entirely but in the same theatre. The face that also went public in 1995 (but nowhere near as public as that of Leah Betts), this time beaming out from an advert for the London listings magazine *Time Out*. The face of an unknown young man showing all the signs of being high on Ecstasy. The face accompanied by the words 'Take Some'. If Leah Betts' is the face of fear, this young man's is one of the many faces of ease. Ease which values Ecstasy for its perceived effects – empathy, openness, well being, heightening of the senses, simply (in the words of many I've interviewed) 'getting bolloxed' or spirituality. Ease which perhaps culturally reflects the unique combined stimulant and relaxant effects, the combined psychedelic and amphetamine pharmacological structure of the drug. Ease still rooted in the early views of Ecstasy as a benign, harmless drug, less destructive and violent than the alcohol so favoured by the official world and less destructive and passive than the heroin so favoured out on the social margins. Ease which *may* flow from the eternal spring of invincibility for so long associated with youth but which is also rooted in valued hedonism and altered states of mind.

While the tabloid moral outrage party rages on and the official world panics about a 'killer drug', one of so many threats to their children in modern times, a world-within-a-world, seemingly invisible but all around us, continues to party on (seemingly) regardless. The first 1996 issue of *Mixmag*, a music and club culture magazine with a circulation of 80,000 (double that of the previous year in a market niche which has trebled in the same year) informed its readers, in a novel interpretation of the distant economic days of the fifties, 'You Never Had It So Good'.

> *Once we were living for the weekend now we're 24 hour party people. Friday/Saturday night flirtation with club culture has become a full-time total commitment. What was once a brief encounter, an occasional, messy one night stand, has become a deep and meaningful relationship. The proliferation of dance music is spreading like a virus, infecting every nook and cranny.*
>
> JAMES, M. QUOTED IN CHAMPION, S. 1990

This writer for the 'hip' youth press was speaking in the earlier days of a scene, many of whose devotees at the time (if anecdotal reports are any kind of reliable indication) have now returned to the occasional Friday or Saturday night flirtation with club culture in 1996, and some of them will have filled their lives with too many other things to keep up what was once 'a deep and meaningful relationship' at all. But 'every nook and cranny' has continued to be 'infected'. The profile of the one million punters per weekend estimated as participating in this hedonistic relationship may have changed (and who knows what percentage of them are experiencing a 'messy one night stand' at any one time) but there is no doubt that 'total commitment' remains in some quarters. As each new generation falls in love, becomes obsessed then begins to settle down and stabilize this hedonistic relationship, another begins its own version. And some never give up.

> *Clubland is not just a place of fun, frills, frolics, flirting and other unmentionables beginning with 'f' y'know. It's also a place of fashion. A place where you can dress up, dress down and flash yourself around. Where heaps of today's top designers nick all their best ideas from and where enough of tomorrow's big designers are already dressing the trendy, the cool, the brave, the foolish and the plain up for it.*
> MIXMAG, 1994

No potatoing on the couch for this crowd. In the year that ended in bitter tears for some and fears for many, events (advertized in any number of national and local magazines as well as record shops, clothes shops, café bars and clubs) across the country offered you the opportunity to get a 'Life' in Manchester, 'Feel' at Preston, taste the 'Flavour' in Edinburgh, 'Love To Be ...' in Sheffield, reap 'Havoc' in Nottingham, go 'Golden' in Stoke-on-Trent, get 'Back To Basics', attend a 'UK Tribal Gathering' in Oxfordshire, witness a 'Renaissance' at a stately home in Warwickshire, 'get your teeth into four succulent rooms' at 'Ripe' in Mansfield, have 'Pure Sex' in Portsmouth or something 'Naughty But Nice!' in Hereford, 'Get Lifted' in Burnley or visit 'The Promised Land' in King's Cross, London. And that's just to name but a handful of the events on offer through the year – comprising what is now a multi-million pound industry. The Henley Centre's report (October 1993) on a study of youth markets estimated consumer spending on raves could now amount to £1.8 billion per annum, putting the market at around the same size as the book or newspaper market and at least a quarter of the spirits market. And that was three years ago. The Premier League 'superclubs' which have grown during that time now shift merchandise like their soccer counterparts and have turnovers well over £1 million. Feel-good factors come and go but, evidently unlike politicians and much of the rest of Britain's adult population, some young people seem to have found one, maintained and sustained it. And all this is just the commercial side of things. The more anti-consumerist youth 'tribes' involved in Free Parties and festivals up and down the land, in country field and urban wasteland, are also committed to partying big time. And they definitely don't go back to the office on Monday (signing on for their dole cheque and buying lottery tickets are about the only ways they are willing to participate in the official world).

Whatever the persuasion of its diverse devotees – consumerist, anti-consumerist, participating in the old social order or committed to 'never coming back' enough to cover their bodies in tattoos and multiple piercings – the signs are that, far from dying, this version of youthful You-Never-Had-It-So-Good based around dancing, music and drugs is growing rather than fading. And the power of this chemical culture is growing in the official world. Look at the success of Quentin Tarantino's film, *Pulp Fiction*, for instance, or Irvine Welsh, the so-called guru of the chemical generation's, *Trainspotting*. *Trainspotting* the book sold 305,000 by early 1996; the film broke box office records and three theatrical adaptations sold out up and down the country. From the chemical generation's point of view, altered mind states and hedonism are as normal as watching 'Coronation Street' or buying a Lottery ticket.

BEYOND FEAR AND EASE: UNCERTAINTY

The secret is out: the adult world has had thrust upon it the attitudes and lifestyle of a generation it does not understand ... one suspects that over the coming months we are going to witness a real drugs war, between a

FEAR, EASE AND BEYOND

bemused mainstream – afraid, anxiously clinging on to their Bristol Cream,
their Valium and their Sunday Express – and an evergrowing group who are
laid back, detached, self-reliant, and take drugs for pleasure. There are two
nations ready for civil war. One is saying 'no', the other is saying 'yes'.

HODGKINSON, 1996

The Ecstasy case is unsolved. That much is clear. But the way I've
been telling it, suggesting it's all one big reciprocal process, I hope
you're beginning to see why. The process seems eternal. The Ecstasy
case is about much, much more than a pill, we all know that if we're
honest. But where the case so far has revolved around declarations of
quick fixes and certainty, my inquiry will embrace uncertainty and
give rein to the urge to Just Say Think.

Don't get me wrong. I'm as much of a certainty addict in many
ways as anyone. After all, my work requires it of me. And where
Ecstasy has been concerned, I've definitely been part of the Just Say
Know brigade. But a particular part of it: the Just Say Know What We
Don't Know bunch. The bunch who feel it's important to admit you
don't have all the answers when the information simply isn't there.
And we actually know very little about Ecstasy. We *should* know more
about its physical and mental effects, who's taking how much, where
and when, etc. It's become increasingly vogue for all in the Ecstasy
case, the majority of politicians excluded, to call for more knowledge.
'Exaggeration starts with an E ... Education starts with an E. It's your
life and your choice. Just say know,' *Mixmag* told Planet Youth in 1992
(Field, 1992). 'In the journey we have taken over these weeks, there is
a lifetime of information that people that can actually change society
should have done,' Paul Betts told ordinary folk in the TV
documentary, *World In Action*, in 1995. 'We're confused and need more
accurate information' was the cry of much of the young audience at
The Guardian's 'E debate' in London in May 1996. Saying Just Say Know
about the drug and its effects is fine – perhaps the single most

interesting fact worth investigating is why Ecstasy-related death was such a peculiarly British phenomenon until recently – but I'll leave that to my colleagues. I happen to think there's no such thing as value-free knowledge and following that line of inquiry takes us back to the trade in certainties. I want to know more about what's behind it all. And it's not just because I do 'social science' for a living. Social science can throw you into the certainty game as much as anything. But I'll give up on certainty for the rest of this book if you will. Even though, in many ways, I've got a lot more to give up.

My past personal experience, for one thing. I remember the mismatch between reading in the sixties about crazed young folk who threw themselves out of windows on LSD trips and who became heroin addicts after smoking 'pot', and my own experience of being with people who took both drugs but did none of these things. My disbelief was not challenged when the majority of these people grew up to be caring and sharing but upright citizens in their way. This experience made me sceptical of all the scary tabloid headlines about what was 'Acid House' in 1988.

This personal scepticism made for a kind of certainty about the Ecstasy case which survived seeing casualties who contacted the drug agency in which I was based for three years, the many stories of bad experiences and problems I collected and the reported deaths. Like Planet Youth, my initial certainty that the whole case was all exaggeration and little foundation was a response to the official moral high ground. These casualties were always exceptions – the people who overdid things by taking too many tablets too often, mixing drugs; the people who had had 'rogue' or 'snide' Ecstasy; the people who had not heeded harm reduction advice; the people who had drunk either not enough or too much water, etc. I empathized with a mass of young people whose culture was being shaped by a drug which itself encouraged empathy, rather than with moral hysteria.

FEAR, EASE AND BEYOND

I still don't have a stomach for hysteria but I'm willing to admit I'm far less easy about it all, far less certain. I'm a parent too. I'm a mid-lifer, I know something of the generation gap from the other side; what the growing reality of having more past than future feels like. Anyone with a scrap of commonsense now knows that taking Ecstasy does present a risk – to your physical and mental health, if nothing else. And even taking it sensibly, observing all the precautions currently available, isn't always enough to protect the taker. But in the end, the same person with common sense also knows that this has little to do with anything in the end. It's not what drug you take, it's who's taking it, where, when, how and why. And it's about what this means to the taker and to everyone else. So, having re-opened the Ecstasy case, I'm going to pursue my line of inquiry which, I hope, already has you looking beyond the drug itself to the meaning it has taken on in Britain in the last decade. We have the uncertainty. We've given up trying to come up with a quick fix. Let's see where it leads us. Let's at least try and turn on and tune in to the broader messages surrounding the new chemical culture and drop out of the vicious cycle we're currently trapped in. Let's Just Say Stop and Think for a while, look fear and ease in the face, instead of running away from or shouting the same things at a phenomenon of 10 years which shows no sign of abating.

4

Drugs 'r' us:
the slippery slope

First let's look at one of the most popular fear/ease scenarios in the Ecstasy case after the current preoccupation with Ecstasy-related death. The certainty on one side is that an illegal drug is a drug is a drug. Ecstasy is heroin (after all, the law says it is). It makes no odds which one, once the young have tried any illegal drug, they'll become addicted. All is equal on the slippery drugs slope. It will all ultimately end in tears. The corresponding certainty on the other side of the generational divide is that Ecstasy is a fun drug. Full stop. So let's look at the certainties and then see how uncertain things really are.

FEAR

Lara died prematurely, before she had the chance to help others. She was a little star that burned too brightly. I hope she will be remembered as the beautiful, funny girl she always was before the drugs changed her forever.
(DERGES, 1996)

March 1996. Another young white female face, pretty and smiling, appears on another front page reporting another drug-related death. This time, it is the death of Lara Derges, a 17-year-old Norwich 'heroin addict', from 'an overdose of anti-depressants'. Some would say a very different death from that of Leah Betts, the face which still dominates the official images of the drug threat. But it *seems* the same – especially to the fearful eye of a parent. Especially because this tragic story is sharing the front page of a regional daily which, on the crest of the new wave of adult fear which began in autumn 1995 and one of many media initiatives during Dealing With Drugs Week in March 1996, commendably took on the responsibility of producing a '16-page special for adults and youngsters'. Seemingly an earnest attempt to present reliable information about drugs to both sides of the Ecstasy hill, to Just Say Know. It also, however inadvertently, replayed the moral outrage party's same old tune. The one which draws all illicitly-used drugs together into the same rhetoric of moral decline and fear.

END OF THE CENTURY DRUG FEAR (RE)MIX: EVERYTHING STARTS WITH AN 'E'

An effortless skimming from one drug to another until they are all one in the big blender of public threat, has played a central role in the popular drugs tale, in the production and maintenance of drug fear. As the above reporting illustrates, concern about Ecstasy, revived to an all-time high by Leah Betts' death, dovetails effortlessly with a concern about all illegal drugs.

The tabloid birth of the Ecstasy media tale in 1988 was only one of many which have fanned fear around drugs in the last decade. But, because it keeps coming back with some regularity, the Ecstasy story has played an important role in holding the drug threat together, in maintaining the pop ethic that all drugs are the same because they all lead to addiction. It has done so through both its uniqueness and its similarity to other drugs. Ecstasy's uniqueness lay in its sexiness both as a 'new' drug (even though it was first patented in 1914 as an appetite suppressant, it wasn't used in the way we have become accustomed to in Britain until the eighties) and as one whose use was widespread, persistent (not the passing craze it was initially viewed as) and apparently socially acceptable to many who frowned upon the use of other Class A drugs. And with a name like Ecstasy the angles were limitless – no other drug went by a name which expressed a feeling of any kind, let alone such an extremely positive one. Its similarity with other drugs was simply that tabloid and other forms of reporting tended to focus on drug-related death, mental problems, etc and employ the same indiscriminate language of addiction. Almost from its inception, the tabloid Ecstasy tale, 'Acid House' in its infant stage, made the connection between Ecstasy and a Class A drug with a very bad press, heroin. 'They may as well call it heroin house,' Rick Astley, the boy-next-door pop-chart crooner of the time was quoted as saying. Addiction was the key lingo: 'Tragic junkies are risking death by using a terrifying new drugs cocktail' warned the Daily Star (Whittow and Edwards, 1988). The collective, look-down-your-moral-nose term, 'drugs', was also key. 'I've never been to an acid house club, but my mate went to one and everyone in the place was out of their heads on drugs,' Matt Goss of Bros, the eighties teenage girl-cum-gay lad heartthrob equivalent of nineties boy group, Take That, told The Sun. Ecstasy, heroin, it's all drugs, it's all the same and it's all bad, sang the boozy tabloid moral outrage revellers and equally boozy Westminster in unison.

The late eighties and the nineties to date have kept this moral-outrage-on-drugs party well stocked. As well as Ecstasy, crack cocaine and heroin have enjoyed more than five minutes of fame but also, to a lesser degree, solvents, LSD, you name it, in fact. In particular, there's been the double whammy of drugs and AIDS. The discovery that the HIV virus could be and was being transmitted through the sharing of needles among heroin users fortified an already virile media vilification of the people first affected by the virus, gay men. Now there was another string to the God Punishes The Immoral bow, so wonderfully articulated by the then Chief Constable of Greater Manchester Police, James Anderton, when he claimed divine inspiration for his controversial speech on AIDS in which he described people as 'swirling around in a cess pit of their own making'. National and local rags carried stories of 'dirty junkies' whose 'dirty needles' were to be found in every nook and cranny of the land (but especially places where innocent children could find them) and of 'junky' prostitutes and mothers who spread their infection to babies and clients like evil harpies.

The popular drugfest has been relentless over the last decade. Turn on the television or radio, read a newspaper or magazine, visit the cinema or rent a video and drugs are part of the landscape. Personal disaster stories, pop- and film-stars, ordinary folk. This drug survey, that drug survey – telling us that more kids are doing more drugs at an ever earlier age. Even the so-called quality press gatecrashed the tabloid moral outrage party, even if they did sit quietly in the kitchen and sneer. Even the most balanced reporting has kept the roadshow rolling. *The Sunday Mirror* may have asked 'What will your kids be doing tonight?' (Thornton, 1994); *The Mail On Sunday* may have shouted that 'Killer drugs flood back' (Stern 1996); but *The Independent* informed us that 'Drug abuse lays waste a generation' (Bennetto, 1994); *The Observer* reported on 'Slaughter by the needle' (Arlidge, 1994) and discussed the question of 'Free will versus the slavery of addiction' (Nelson, 1994). *Guardian* readers learned that 'More than 50 per cent of 16 to 21 year olds know how and where to buy drugs on the street, in their schools, college and at clubs, a Gallup survey for the YMCA revealed' (Bunting, 1994); 'Drugs offences are rising faster in many rural areas than in inner cities.

Even the smallest hamlets are affected' (Friend, 1994) and were
warned of 'Drugs fear for under-11s' (Brindle, 1996). The huge public
hype surrounding the film of Irvine Welsh's book, *Trainspotting*, only
served to pile on the agony – which was on the up anyway with
reports suggesting that heroin, the ultimate bogey drug, was making
a comeback (Travis, 1996).

This fevered media overload has now become tired and tiresome.
However much popular fears take on the quality of so much
background noise in many lives as a result, the fear of drugs is not
going away and Ecstasy is at its centre, still highly symbolic of
widespread drug use among young people and of the slippery slope of
drugs. One puff on a cannabis joint, one tablet of Ecstasy and the
inevitable slippery slope to addiction, dereliction and death begins.
No wonder Planet Middle Age is frightened and wants to take control,
parent and protect the babies.

EASE

EEZER GOODE: ECSTASY ON HONEYMOON

To view things from the other side of the Ecstasy generational
divide, we need to go back to the early days when this mythical drug
got together with house music and large indoor and outdoor public
spaces in Britain, to understand a key root of Planet Youth's seeming
Ease. Picture, if you will, the late eighties. You read the papers and
magazines which talk of the dangers of a new drug but one which
promises much in its name alone. One which supposedly makes you
feel happy, confident, loving towards others, exhilarated, sexy even. It
doesn't have a come-down or any of the fear or anxiety associated
with LSD. You can't get addicted. One of your friends tries it first and
describes to you the best feelings since sliced bread. You finally try

one and enter a sensual pleasure landscape much bigger and so much longer-lasting than any club you've ever set foot in before. Complete strangers, often from a completely different social group than your own, become your instant friends. Anxiety and self-consciousness are out of the window. Ecstasy is something that allows you to share the most amazing experiences and feel like you belong with hundreds or thousands of other people more than you ever did before. Like one of the first Ecstasy 'experts' with a foothold in both the 'hip' youth magazines and the drug policy and service arena put it:

> Individuals develop a strange relationship with Ecstasy, a different relationship than with other drugs. Because they have such a good time on Ecstasy and it makes them feel so benevolent, there's a sense of 'Well, this isn't a drug, or, if it is, it's a very benign substance.'
> MCDERMOTT, 1991

Of all the interviews I've conducted, this 17-year-old woman's description of the experience is still the one which seems to capture what all the other people, many older and/or more educated than her, I've talked to have attempted to convey – yet few have been able to put into words (dissolving into physical expressions and gestures instead). In 1992 when I interviewed her in Manchester, she valued the experience of going to what were called 'raves' at the time more highly than sex – which she also enjoyed:

> The first time I took it I thought to myself it's like being in heaven, that's the only thing I could think of. It was like when you listen to music, you know that the music is coming out of the speakers but when you're on 'E', it's like you're not dancing on the floor, you're dancing on the notes and the music is all around you and it's like dancing with you and you feel so up there it's like, erm, it's so hard to describe, it's just like heaven and you just feel so

good and you love everybody. You just look round and think 'Oh you're all wonderful. It's such a wonderful atmosphere. DJ you're wonderful'. And you get a really good song on and you get like the vibes going through your body and erm like rushes and that's when everybody starts screaming and raving on. We just feel so great about ourselves it's er fantastic. I've never felt anything like it in my life.

Who but the stiffest of British youth could listen to that and not be vaguely interested? In its honeymoon period in Britain, Ecstasy didn't need the additional marketing of the tabloid press and other media hype. Once tried, this product became a brand leader. But by golly the extra free marketing did it good.

While Ecstasy was still on honeymoon in Britain, users singled it out from others as being different. It was the one. They were anti-alcohol, the drug so acceptable to the mainstream. Sipping on Lucozade and mineral water, sneering at 'beer monsters' who didn't know how to enjoy themselves and who sadly paraded in the meat-market discos, throwing up after a curry or in the back of a taxi and fumbling with some stranger they could not recall the morning after. They were also anti-heroin – addiction, going on the nod, a life devoted to acquiring a drug that kept you down and out forever were for sad 'junkies' and 'skagheads'. To them this was a universe away from the happy daze of 'E' which broke through all the social boundaries, uniting plumbers, estate agents, scallies, hooray henrys, McJobbers, bank clerks, secretaries, students, dole slackers, doctors and nurses, office cleaners, social workers and teachers, football players and hooligans alike on the same Luvdup 'vibe'. To them Ecstasy was part of a whole social scene, in which cannabis was smoked like fags and many users didn't even know Ecstasy was a Class A drug in the eyes of the law. Part of an emerging culture. A culture which was not about taking control but letting go. Letting the music and movement take control. Taking an excursion into a world

of sensuality and altered mind states. While one side of the
generational divide were worried about the psychological effects of
drugs, the other side were shouting 'mental, mental' en masse, even
calling themselves 'ravers'. To them 'mad' was a positive expression,
freeing and feeding the mind in a way the moral high grounders
could not begin to imagine was a way of life. From this side of the
Ecstasy hill, the slippery drugs slope meant nothing but a bad come-
down, the equivalent of hangover. Forget the face of the leading
character in this musical, it had a cast of millions.

INTO UNCERTAINTY

Moving beyond these two certainties, which consistently feed
one another in the Ecstasy case, seems a physical impossibility in the
public arena. The eternal cycle of quick-fix versus no-fix-required will
probably grind on. But giving up certainty and following my line of
inquiry may give you a less reassuring but more realistic account of
where post-modern high times are really at. Ultimately, it is too early
to predict if it will all end in tears (or what kind of tears they may be)
but there are a few things we need to Just Say Think about if we are
interested in moving beyond the drugs, and particularly Ecstasy,
impasse at all.

PICK 'N' MIX IN THE DRUGS SWEETSHOP

First of all, the Ecstasy honeymoon has long been over within
the culture. The picture of Ecstasy use in Britain painted by the few
studies carried out suggest a typical pattern of individual use which
begins with a honeymoon period of high benefits from the drug with
little cost, followed by increased cost and increased consumption to
get the previous level of benefit. Just like this individual pattern of

use, Ecstasy use in Britain has emerged from its honeymoon period. In fact, the new chemical generation began to play the field before the honeymoon was over. The culture with a drug which encouraged empathy, love to one's fellow human beings, a feeling of belonging at its heart, also opened its arms to pills, pints and powder. Fluctuations in the supply and perception of the quality of the drug among users have taken their toll (as well as the basic instinct of boredom by all accounts – eternal well-being on a Saturday night is, it would seem, hard to sustain).

Alcohol is back on the drug menu in many clubs and parties and has been for some time. LSD and amphetamines were on the list from the early days and it's been snowing cocaine in cities and towns up and down the country for some time (a recent study of banknotes found that 40 per cent had traces of cocaine). Temazepam, other tranquilizers and opiates such as heroin and methadone have been reported as joining cannabis on the list of 'comedown' drugs. What is more, if the sexual attraction of Ecstasy isn't what it was, the romance is still there. The culture the now-not-necessarily-so-harmless pill helped create is still full of chemical promise for new generations who still want a slice of the action and want to buy into the concept of Ecstasy. 'Probably the biggest Ecstasy survey ever' in Britain, conducted by *Mixmag* and the Manchester-based Lifeline (Drugs) Project, suggested that more people are trying Ecstasy for the first time every year. Nearly a quarter of the 4,003 respondents who used Ecstasy began doing so in 1994, long after the 'hip' underground said it was over, and nearly another quarter began doing so in 1995. Despite ailments like boils, backache, vomiting, blackouts; despite the panic attacks; despite the bogus or 'snide' tablets and the oft-perceived low quality of tablets; despite the job losses and ructions with friends and family; despite the prison terms served by mates who were only stocking up on tablets for the weekend group outing; despite the deaths; and especially despite (or to spite, even) the official world's fear, Ecstasy is still part of the end of the century chemical romance. 'From here to eternity and back to the office on Monday' and 'Thank f**k it's Friday' still apply. And Drugs 'R' Us really is included on Planet Youth's shopping trip. If it's normal to be afraid of all drugs on one side of the Ecstasy hill, on the other 'Drugs 'R' (now) Us'. Ecstasy is a normal part of life, a positive lifestyle bonus, as much a part of a good night out as deodorizing your pits or buying a pair of silver PVC hipsters; a form of social cement in these post-modern times; a balance sheet on which the benefits still outweigh the costs.

I, for one, have little doubt that Ecstasy has been at the centre of the expansion of the illicit drug market, at the heart of the new relationship between young people and drugs. It is the one we look at now when we refer to dance drug/Ecstasy/house culture, together with the broader group, dubbed the 'post-heroin generation' by drugs researchers – which also includes kids mostly too young to go to clubs and parties. The huge amount of media hype the 'Love' or 'Hug' drug has received both over- and underground in the last decade made it sexy and helped keep it that way. But the special relationship with Ecstasy as a harmless, weekend party drug opened up a whole new range of people to chemical romance who may previously never have entered the illicit drug world. If Planet Middle Age talk only of 'drugs', some on Planet Youth request only a 'tablet' or 'pill' when making their purchase for a night out. They're buying a drug concept, rather than a specific drug with known and consistent effects (Forsyth, 1995).

My own and other studies (e.g. Henderson, 1993a and b; Parker et al, 1995; Coffield and Gofton, 1994) only confirm what is obvious if you go to a 'dance' club or event, read the growing number of music magazines or favourites like *Loaded* (the British lad's magazine of the nineties); listen to song lyrics, or look at their titles. There are even blatant drug references in adverts (e.g. the latest ad for BT rival,

Ionica, blatantly makes visual drug references to those 'in the know', as white doves (the Ecstasy connoisseur's brand name) fly, the viewer is told, 'You can feel it' and the whole ad is shot in surreal drug-inspired colour) and on innumerable T-shirts and items of clothing (forget 'Beanz Meanz Heinz' and 'Kit-E-Kat', it's been 'Heinz Meanz Eaz' and 'HipEKat', and 'Spliffy' label clothes for kids, for some time). By the end of a two-year project in Manchester (at the end of 1993), I was convinced of at least one thing: illegal drugs, alcohol and cigarettes are part of a range of consumer products (relating to music, style and fashion) through which young people buy into a lifestyle, in many ways public but also (generationally speaking) private. A lifestyle in which a 'pick 'n' mix' attitude to life in general includes drugs. A bit of this, a bit of that and you can compose your life in a decomposing world. (Less frequently, perhaps, illegal drugs, alcohol and cigarettes are also among the few consumer products acceptable to the new protest cultures wishing to escape the official consumerist world and live life on the margins, cobbling together a lifestyle out of fragments from centuries past and present.)

Coffield and Gofton found that, although young people cannot be regarded as an homogeneous group and there is a distinct segmentation in the market for their leisure services: 'young people approach soft drugs in the same rational, matter-of-fact way they deal with other consumer goods.' The authors of a much-quoted report, 'Drugs Futures', noted that 'illegal drugs have become products which are grown, manufactured, packaged and marketed through an enterprise culture whereby the legitimate and illicit drug markets have merged. Thus if people wish to purchase psychoactive experiences, "time out" or even oblivion, then they are able to do so' and found that young people with a pick 'n' mix attitude to drug-taking 'appear to be less concerned with peer group status and more with rational consumption as part of (their) approach to leisure time. This suggests that the prevalence of drug use will be sustained and normalised towards the year 2,000' (Parker et al, 1996). It was what most of us involved in research on the new chemical culture have been saying in the nineties.

BACK TO BASICS: IS 'NO PROBLEM' A PROBLEM?

So it's not just Ecstasy but a whole range of drugs involved in the new chemical culture. This much ordinary folk drawn to the moral high ground assumed – and they're increasingly proved right. The latest studies tell us that there's been a dramatic increase in drug use even since 1992. Half of all men aged between 16 and 29 years told the British Crime Survey (a survey of 10,000 people in England and Wales) they had taken drugs at some time – up 50 per cent on the figures in the 1992 study (Ramsay and Percy, 1996). Meanwhile, in the Health Education Authority's study of over 5,000 11 to 35 year olds in 1995, 45 per cent had taken an illegal drug, rising to over 60 per cent for 20 to 22 year olds (Health Education Authority, 1996). Perhaps the kids really are innocently courting disaster? Well, it's more complicated than that if we stay steadfastly in the uncertainty zone. For starters, it's wrong to think that the chemical generation doesn't think there is no problem with all this chemical excess.

'It's normal,' they tell us researchers and the TV cameras. And in many ways, to them, it is. It's no big deal. Pick up your fags, your vitamin C, your bananas or whatever and your 'something for the weekend' in pill or powder form. Deal with the comedown, even if it feels like a major life crisis. It's life. The state and the official world don't come into it.

It's been part of my work in recent years to go around different parts of the country asking Planet Youth about drug problems relating to the new chemical generation – however and/or whether they perceive them. Sure, I've heard the official 'no problem' version time and time again but if you begin to dig a little, 'problem' does get defined, and always in spookily, over-the-other-side-of-the-Ecstasy-hill-speak, as 'addiction'. What they actually mean by this term is, however, something rather different to the moral outrage version. They're referring to the ones who spend all their time sitting around getting stoned, who get depressed and grouchy without cannabis. The ones with amphetamine psychosis. The ones who get so greedy with their Saturday night fever, it carries on long into the week and panic attacks, paranoia, uncontrollably shaking limbs, hospitalization in a state of hyperventilation, or seizure even, follow. They lose their jobs, don't get on with their school or college work, don't get on with the business of robbing car stereos, computer chips, etc, or coming off the dole. If there are those who, like the young woman I quoted earlier, want to stay in the purist 'E' honeymoon period, there are 'dribbling messes' – with 'head lolling, tongue hanging out, can't talk and stuff' who 'give the rest of us a bad name' (as one young woman put it recently) and 'drug bores' in a dance culture of excess:

> Nobody ever told us about the dangers of drug bores to our social life. These are the people who live every weekend like it was their last, spend all their excess cash on popping pills, hoovering lines and knocking back narcotics like it was going out of fashion. You'll find them slumped in corners of clubs, draped over bars or locked in your toilet at post-club sessions. They don't want to dance, they don't want to get to know you, they don't even seem to want to enjoy themselves any more. They just want to flake out and forget ... Excuse me while I crack my jaw yawning ... let's be frank, drug bores are a depressing sign of the times. A gripping recession means most of us now live for the weekends, and five years of hedonism are bound to claim a few victims. But what a way to go.
>
> I-D (JAMES, 1993)

There has been uncertainty in the youthful world-within-a-world for some time. The concerns which began to be voiced to me in interviews from 1991 onwards were also voiced in magazines:

> Enthusiasm for Ecstasy may be starting to wane. People have begun to notice that the initial pleasure can give way to spiritual and psychological disruption. Fear about the impact of Ecstasy on health is growing. Some 20 people have died after taking 'E' in the UK over the last two years. Other problems associated with the drug are still emerging ... Personally I'm bored with feeling so nice every Saturday night.
>
> THE FACE (MCDERMOTT, 1991)

'Has the Nightmare Begun?' asked Mixmag in 1993:

> 500,000 ecstasy tablets going down people's necks every weekend. And it's been like that for at least three years now. Ecstasy, speed, cocaine, acid, even Ketamine, and all of it burning up clubland ... Now it would seem that some of the results are coming in. Some long-term drug users are complaining of serious psychological damage. Paranoia, panic attacks, hallucinations, pissing blood. It seems unlikely that every drug user will be affected but for the party people interviewed here it has proved all too easy to burn out on drugs.
>
> DIXON, 1993

Some say that drugs are drugs and Planet Youth is doomed. Some say 'Drug 'R' Us', no problem. But I say there is a problem. It's just not like the moral high ground loves to tell it. I've been told time and time again that Ecstasy is, like chocolate, a culturally (as opposed to pharmacologically) 'morish' drug. Its own special effects within the house culture environment helped create a culture of excess. You want more of the whole cultural experience, of which the drug is just one part. Now that drug markets have responded to the new demand and diversified, culturE has found that treating other drugs the same way *can* cause problems. Multi-drug cocktails during the course of a weekend, hammering cocaine like there's no tomorrow, simply taking Ecstasy even, *can* and does lead to all kinds of problems. Apart from severe financial and legal ones, your physical and mental health can and do suffer. To deny this is either playing the devil's advocate or the fool. How these drug-related costs compare with the costs related to alcohol, tobacco and other state-sponsored drugs is currently anyone's guess. It's too soon to know for sure. Existing statistics on relative costs in terms of death suggest that the state is sponsoring the more dangerous drugs. But death is the terminal of a range of problems.

BACK TO BASICS: CANNABIS IS NOT HEROIN (REVISITED): I

Let's be clear, acknowledging that there are drug-related problems in the new chemical culture doesn't mean joining the moral outrage party and assuming that the chemical generation are inevitably doomed. There may be tears of regret along the way as ever scarcer jobs, further/higher education and other career opportunities get inadvertently shelved in favour of short-term pleasures. There may be tears of regret as immune systems, body weights, menstrual cycles, general abilities to cope with the everyday business of the modern world, friends and family, general mental balance go awry. But, although contemporary youth drugs-a-go-go may not be entirely unproblematic, it won't necessarily all end up with the kind of dereliction we associate with heroin.

I'm one of the bunch on Planet Middle Age who remembers how the 'all is equal on the slippery drugs slope' chestnut felt in the days when drugs first hit a mass youth market (albeit on a much smaller scale than today). Then it was the 'pot'-to-heroin thesis – hotly contested on both sides of the Atlantic in the sixties and early seventies. Sociologists and some new 'drug experts', many of whom, we can only surmise, themselves moved (or had moved) in cultures where 'pot' was an acceptable social drug, attempted to prove that there was no causal link by basically pointing out that only a small proportion of cannabis smokers become heroin users. Their sparring partners were those who argued the converse: that most heroin users have smoked cannabis. The 'slippery slope' theory was actually another American import – first muted in the thirties in the face of 'Reefer Madness', the tabloid drug-crazed youth hell of the time. Federal anti-marijuana legislation was first passed by US Congress in 1937 and was based on the views expressed in expert testimony at hearings held that same year, i.e. that reefer-smoking led to evil: murder, rape, robbery, insanity, brain damage and suicide. Expert testimony of the following kind:

> Marijuana users easily … become engulfed in the abyss of drug addiction, and end their miserable existence either on the gallows, or in penal institutions and insane asylums. The moral and physical resistance to narcotics and alcohol is not only weakened but often destroyed in persons of stabilised personality, who are addicted, even to a moderate degree, to marijuana.
>
> FOSSIER, 1931

In 1969, the Wootton Report sent a strong message to the British public – 'cannabis is not heroin' (Wootton, 1969). Its primary purpose, to discourage 'the draconian and probably ineffective practice of sending people to prison for use of a drug that is pharmacologically less harmful than alcohol' (Wade, 1969) has been achieved in some ways since the 1971 Misuse of Drugs Act distinguished between cannabis (Class B) and heroin and cocaine (Class A). But the slippery slope instinct lives on. I still find it hard to swallow now. For one thing, it begins with a 'starter drug' (once cannabis, now, in the nineties, any drug viewed as recreational by its users) and ends with heroin in a narrative of moral decline – but straightforward narratives of any kind are fading in this post-modern world. For another, I, like many others between the age of 40 and 60-odd, actually know or have been acquainted with punters from that first mainstream chemical generation in a consumer society who, a bit like the supposedly rational drug consumers of today, differentiated between drugs, gave them different cultural value. They rarely went beyond their drugs of choice (mainly psychedelics of various kinds and marijuana), or if they did, it wasn't a long and lasting relationship. The majority went on to be useful members of society. For yet another thing, although we don't have a major national longitudinal study of Ecstasy use in Britain, my own and other researchers' and drug workers' experience and anecdotal evidence, as the people in the official world with contact with various groups within culturE over any substantial period of time, suggests a typical Ecstasy career which peaks early and tails off. A sizable chunk of the chemical generation appear to be following drug pathways where an initial honeymoon period (lasting anything from a few weeks or months to a few years) in which the lifestyle takes over and dwarfs other dimensions of life, usually comes to an end and what used to be a case of living for the weekend, becomes just another fun Saturday night out. Or gets replaced entirely.

BACK TO BASICS: CANNABIS IS NOT HEROIN (REVISITED): II

It's worth pursuing the question of heroin addiction and death as the inevitable end for the new chemical generation further. Sixties 'soft' and 'hard' drugs-speak stays with us in the nineties even though the categories don't match current or previous legal categories. Ecstasy is a Class A drug like heroin but is still considered 'soft' by those with an eye to relative drug harms. What the terms 'hard' and 'soft' aimed to describe was the place of certain drugs within different cultures and lifestyles. A more modern equivalent, fashionable in some circles, distinguishes between two main groups of drug users: one very large and mainly recreational in which drugs are an adjunct to fun; one much smaller involving drug dependence, where drugs are the central organizing feature of life and injecting is the norm. This clarification is usually instantly muddied in the minds of common people, thanks to sociological tendencies born of a desire to turn the moral volume down, which label the former 'Group B' and the latter 'Group A' (Gilman, 1992). So, to make things easier, I'll rename 'Group A' drug users as 'the careerists' and 'Group B' as 'the hobbyists and part-timers'.

It's worth noting that drug careerists are keen to distinguish themselves from the hobbyists too. An obvious recent example of this lies in cyberspace – when 'Alt.drugs' appeared on the Internet, it swiftly sub-divided into 'Alt.drugs.hard' and 'Alt.drugs.soft'. The hobbyists and part-timers are equally keen to distance themselves. The early anti-alcohol ethic within the new chemical culture may have been eroded over time, although it still exists in some quarters (I think we hear it spoken most among the latest Ecstasy recruits at any given time), but the anti-heroin ethic has been more resistant. In 1992, my interviewees injected disdainful comments about 'dirty junkies' into the conversation without my invitation. Even this girl from East Manchester with a 'junkie' boyfriend sang the same tune:

> It wrecks me when he's smacked up but it doesn't bother me when he's 'E'd up 'cos heroin is a dirty habit and I think, once you're hooked, you're fucked. But 'E's are just weekend tackle.

In 1996, the stories were the same. And in the few cases where I came across people whose fellow part-timer friends had begun using heroin, they couldn't get away fast enough. These friends became ex-friends overnight. In the most recent study I've been working on, which involved collecting 14 to 25 year olds' views on drug availability and use in their area of the country and county, only the tiniest of minorities mentioned heroin. Even when the area they lived in was known (by other researchers) to sport a heroin culture. So in some ways heroin is still a hidden culture. There's a real cultural boundary between it and the other 'Drugs 'R' Us' world.

BACK TO BASICS: BUT WILL IT ALL END IN HEROIN?

So there's a great deal of cause for hope. The new chemical culture isn't nosediving wholesale into the harsh and horrible world we now associate with heroin. Is it? This is where things get complicated. It's one (very important) thing to say there are two very different groups of drug users in Britain today and to differentiate between various drugs and levels of drug-related problem. It's quite another to suggest this is the end of the story. In reality, a clear boundary between drug careerist and part-timer cultures is only a convenient conceptual one.

Look at mainstream popular culture and you'll see it has been rife with junk culture over the last few years. Fashion spreads sport bony young women and men with pale faces and dark eyes, slumped and wasted-looking. 1995 saw reports of both new 'Yuppie' heroin users, 'the junkies of Wall Street', (who, more knowingly than Uma Thurman in *Pulp Fiction*, moved on from cocaine) and a glut of heroin-related deaths. *The Big Issue*, the magazine sold by Britain's homeless, recently reported on an explosion in heroin use, pointing out that heroin seizures have risen consistently throughout the eighties and nineties to last year's record of over a ton (Johnston, 1995–6). A recent article in one of the trade journals of the drug policy and service field, *Druglink*, reported on interviews with 'drug workers' nationally which suggested that 'fall-out from the rave generation', or 'E' casualties, are one of three new groups (other than the ageing group of established heroin users) currently taking to derivatives of the opium poppy (Shapiro, 1996). I know for a fact that our friends in the north at the Lifeline Project were coming across such people as early as 1993. Meanwhile, another recent study concluded that *belief* among users that most Ecstasy contains other drugs including heroin (not fact), may make the transition to these drugs more acceptable (Forsyth, 1995). And style mag, *i-D*, warned last November that:

> *Heroin kills two people every week in Glasgow. It's the most common street drug in Manchester. In London clubbers are using it to chill out. After skipping a generation of recreational drug users, smack is back – and it's more dangerous than ever ... Heroin sells, even as it kills.*
> CORRIGAN, 1995

Even some among the chemical generation are uncertain. Over the last year, I've heard a number of worries about shifting drug standards and 'cut-off' points. Although the order of this young woman's drug experimenting and its extent is not generalizable to chemical culture as a whole, her concerns are typical:

> *First it was, 'I'll smoke but I won't do trips'. Then a few years later I was doing trips but, 'I'm not doing an 'E' '. Then a few weeks later ... Then it was, 'Definitely won't do speed', then I was doing that. Then somebody came round with some opium and so I did it. It disappointed me to think about how I was two years ago and how your standards do change because of what people are doing around you ... Even though I say, like, I don't think I'll do coke, I can't be one hundred per cent sure because people are starting to take a lot more around me now and I wonder about it.*

ECSTASY: CASE UNSOLVED

Having said there is no such thing as the slippery drugs slope like
the moral outrage party tell it, I can't in all honesty say that drug
hobbyists and part-timers never become careerists. Of course people
will always take drugs, including state-sponsored ones, to sink into
oblivion. How many alcoholics do you know of, even if you manage to
by-pass all the 'Trainspotting' multi-drug (and crime) careerists that
are a feature of modern British life? Meanwhile, of course, kids as
young as 13 are into heroin, having tried no other illegal drugs. But
the million dollar question is *how many* use drugs now to get as far
away from it all *all, or much, of the time* and how many more will in
the future?

LIVING LARGE ON A LEAKY BARGE

I started my new line of inquiry from the standpoint of
uncertainty by saying it's too soon to tell if all this drug-taking will
inevitably end in tears for everyone. Ultimately it is. But we in Britain
have been too happy breastbeating and shouting that it will. We
haven't been interested in really trying to find out. It wasn't until 1995
that the government's drugs strategy for England, 'Tackling Drugs
Together' publicly recognized the need to know what's happening
over time. Even still, big national studies of the different pathways
the post-Ecstasy generation are following through the chemical
culture – which listen in-depth to the stories these young people have
to tell – are, to my knowledge, non-existent. We seem to be much
happier to dance to the tune of moral and political rhetoric, to stay in
the safe-houses of fEar and Ease. So, for now, I can only surmise.

If I still have any certainty left, it is that the first wave of
recreational drug-taking in a consumer society in the sixties delivered
unto us only a small percentage of obvious casualties. (Although
thirty years on, we still don't really know the full story – we're still
discovering the full impact of the Second World War on our family

dynamics and internal workings). I'm less sure about today's much bigger chemical culture. In the sixties, there were jobs to return to if you tuned in, turned on and dropped out. There was a feeling that you could take health care, education, a better future than your parents had for granted. Now it's a different scenario altogether. Now dropping out is often not a choice, you have to struggle to drop in. The future has a definite feel-bad air hanging over it for many, despite attempts by politicians of all colours to convince us otherwise. Live, socialize and become a drug hobbyist in the chronically deprived 'Trainspotting' urban areas of Britain and the odds on turning full-time careerist would seem that much higher than doing the same in Knightsbridge. In the drugs career structure, the size of your cultural 'wad' may not be everything (remember the heroin addicts from privileged backgrounds) but it sure does matter.

If it does all end in tears, it won't ultimately be the drugs to blame. Just Say Think.

5

Sex, drugs and the modern girl

If just saying no to certainty allows us to see beyond popular opposition between fear and ease about Ecstasy-related death and about the slippery drugs slope, it can also take us a lot further. Staying with uncertainty isn't easy. We all need its comfort. But gird your loins and follow me, in the next two chapters, into the genderscape of the Ecstasy case. It's an intriguing line of inquiry.

FEAR

This is the smiling face of the devil ... Acid House regalia and a 'Smiley' badge hide the crown of thorns on the plaster figure of Christ on the cross ... Nothing is sacred to this warped drug cult ... Now there are cynical, evil people who are using Jesus to draw in other victims.
THE POST (WILLIAMS, 1988)

It's autumn 1988. The nation is warned of a new 'warped drug cult'. 'Smiley', the logo adopted from earlier drug-happy days by Acid House culture, becomes the new face of threat. In its tabloid version, the face represents the 'evil calling cards' of the sinister drug dealers and party organizers. Along with sinister 'Smiley' came its innocent victim, the leading character in the drugs melodrama ever since – the single white female. Prone and helpless, she is preyed upon by men with evil intent. And in 1988, drugs and pleasure were portrayed as mere 'tricks', 'traps' and 'lures' to entice her into sexual danger.

SEX, DRUGS AND DANCING DAMSELS IN THE ACID HOUSE OF HORROR

When Acid House first made its debut in the tabloids, it was portrayed merely as the latest version of youthful sex, drugs and rock 'n' roll. Readers of *The Sun* were even given the chance to buy the T-shirt and learn the 'lingo' of this 'groovy and cool' new youth cult. But not for long. (Not beyond its music page anyway.) It finally responded to months of egging on from the music press a week later and 'The evil of Ecstasy' was exposed in a full-page spread. Throughout autumn 1988 the tabloid portrait of Acid House was etched along sinister, demonic lines. Acid House party punters were pagan 'revellers' at 'sex-and-drugs orgies'; drug dealers and party organizers were Acid House 'Mr Bigs' who preyed on their victims by seducing them with 'killer music', Ecstasy and other 'mindbending' 'sex drugs' with 'devastating' effects; and 'Smiley', their sinister calling card (Redhead, 1993). This tabloid bacchanal climaxed at the end of October, as the first sacrificial victim was delivered – Janet Mayes, 21-year-old Essex girl, who died after collapsing at an Acid House disco in Surrey.

At first, 'Sex romps', the 'sex' drug and 'sex orgies' were only the broader backdrop to the developing female victim role. Sexual threat mostly only lingered in the air as *The Sun* reported on '14 year old Jenny's' first Ecstasy experience and *The Mirror* gave the low-down on how young girls actually rolled cannabis joints and took LSD. Some more obvious sexual interest was already being aroused, however:

> *Teenage pill-poppers hooked on the Acid house music craze are trying out a new 'love drug' nick-named Fantasy. The stimulant creates a feeling of energy and encourages promiscuity ... One drugs squad detective said last night: '... We fear young girls who are tempted to use it will be taken advantage of by older youths and men.'*
> THE DAILY EXPRESS (TWOMEY, 1988)

By the end of November the tabloid moral outrage party had exposed itself in full leering glory. 'Acid fiends spike Page Three girl's drink' screamed *The Sun* (1988). One of their very own busty beauties had delivered unto them the opportunity to come right out and say it loud and clear – Acid House spelled danger not only from mindbending drugs but also sex for its prime victim – the single white female. The story added 'Spanish men' to the evil rogues gallery. Men who spiked girls' drinks and 'would lie in wait and rape them'. 'Apart from the rape attempt, the worst thing was hallucinating about those ants,' said Tracy Kirby, the Page Three girl in question (Redhead, 1993).

The danger from sex facing the single white female was never spelled out so clearly again. The landscape of fear surrounding the nation's young womanhood has cast many a single white female in an ongoing saga of tragedy, and the corruption of everyday normality and innocence. Tragic tales of normal everyday daughters of normal everyday folk have continually made the headlines: 'Paula never had anything stronger than Diet Coke. Then she took one Ecstasy Pill and it killed her' sang the headlines in summer 1992 (Reed, 1992), in a year when the (now) 'rave' scene was part and parcel of popular culture. In typical style, the story described the 20 year old from Manchester as a 'normal young woman who was a trainee hairdresser, planning to get engaged to her boyfriend, liked doing jigsaws in the evening, could not resist the black kitten in the pet shop and who would spend her last pound on a present for a friend'. She went out for a rare night out to a club with her girlfriend and somehow – the possibility of her drink being 'spiked' was insinuated – took a tablet, had two heart attacks and died. The 'Femail Testimony' page of *The Daily Mail* in spring 1991 told of a father who had to rescue his daughter who was 'sucked into a drugs culture' when her drink was, once more, 'spiked', and take her home and put her to bed 'as though she were a child again'. The 1988 Page Three girl story had a 1992 equivalent in the 'TV flake girl' saga, which saw a model, famous after featuring in a chocolate bar advert lying in a bath in a luxurious room in Venice and lingering over the chocolate in a thinly veiled reference to oral sex, confined to a psychiatric ward after her drink was, once again, allegedly 'spiked' at a party (Hadfield, 1992).

But the explicit threat of sex gave way to wider concerns about the psychological and mortal effects of Ecstasy on our tragic, innocent heroine in an evil drug underworld. 1994 saw a half-hearted attempt to get it up again when it looked like 'GHB' (or, more popularly, 'GBH'), an anaesthetic associated with the death of Hollywood heartthrob, River Phoenix, might prove the next 'sex pill' to sweep Britain's youth high spots. But the wilt set in.

EASE

SHUT UP AND DANCE: BIG TIME SENSUALITY ON THE 'E' HONEYMOON: I

Oddly enough, when the moral panic was more straightforwardly about danger from sex in the late eighties, it was the last thing 'E' types were concerned about in the party zone in 'the Summer of Love' of 1988 and for a few years (especially summers) to come. Group feeling, sensation, non-verbal communication – with dance movements, facial and hand expressions, massage, roaring when the empathy between the crowd, the DJ and high points in the music peaked; a whole host of visual, aural and oral stimuli; serious sweatiness; a social space on a grand scale – were some of the many things on offer, as a growing culture brought more and more, usually conflicting or mutually indifferent, youth tribes together in euphoria. And it was very attractive to girls weary of dance-around-your-handbag, do-the-walk-around-slowly-dance-at-midnight nights out. The girls (aged between 15 and 25 years old) I interviewed in the North West of England between October 1991 and 1993 varied in how often, many, much and long they used Ecstasy, amphetamine and LSD (from three months to three years, mostly on a weekly basis). The majority smoked fags and spliffs on a regular basis and had little taste for alcohol. They came from a range of class, race and ethnic backgrounds and 'went out' (the ubiquitous phrase for attending what were then called 'raves') with a mixed or single-gender crowd of friends. They speak their Ease far better than I:

> When I took 'E' in the beginning, it was a new thing ... travelling in convoys on motorways trying to find the parties dressed in mad, casual clothes ... People travelled from all over the country to be there. Everybody wanted to know one another, it was so exciting ... I used to get up on the speakers and

get the crowd going ... I got these euphoric rushes through my body ... I just wanted to love everybody ... I lived for the weekend just to experience that feeling again, the whole atmosphere.

I love every aspect of this scene. I love the clothes especially. I think that since I started having such brilliant weekends I've made an effort in other parts of my life. I look after myself as much as possible during the week and keep my room tidy. It's all down to 'E', you see things in a different light – mum doesn't know this though!

A lot of girls who go to 'raves' are looking for something different ... they take it more easy with the drugs but they do seem to get a better buzz you know ... I can walk past a lot of people when I'm 'E'ing, a lot of lads, and they won't give me a buzz you know. A lot of them have, like, shady faces and stuff but more girls are dead friendly ... Lads seem to be more tied up in their own field ... They don't seem to sort of give out as much I've noticed ... I think girls go out there to give everybody a buzz. They look round for people more when they're dancing, you know, smile more. They seem like they want to put their love across more than what the lads do.

With really good 'E's, I mean at a really good club, you're just dancing on totally sort of a sexual high. It's just something totally incredible. The dancing and being in the club, that high is what it's all about – and you just don't get it anywhere else, in any shape or form.

The thing I remember is the second time I took 'E' at a club ... I was in a near orgasmic state ... I remember, like, looking round as if I was like saying with my eyes, 'Ah this is what it's like!' but it felt like everyone was going, 'Eiow this is what it's like!' – they all knew ... I can't remember if I came or not but for a long time I was like really just about to and it was just brilliant really.

It's more of an all-over orgasm. It's been too much before. In fact I've had to run off and go and be sick. It was just one of those nights that everything was absolutely wonderful and just dancing quite close and any physical contact, it was just getting higher and higher and higher that suddenly it was too much and I had to run off fairly quickly.

We do fancy blokes at raves and enjoy flirting with them … but it's like going back to when you were younger, you don't want to get them into bed, you're just friendly.

Music, drugs, dancing, social interaction by the shed load, a feeling of belonging, style and fashion – it was all there. The girls I spoke to found it hard to identify which they liked most (sounds and body language took over from words when they were trying to describe the experience). All this sensuality, hedonism, excitement; all this striding around huge social gatherings on your own (often in a small amount of clothing); *and* some spotty, beery fat bloke wasn't going to grope you when all you wanted to do was dance! No wonder so many girls loved it (it was the reason I'd loved gay clubs for years and, interestingly, a lot of girls I interviewed frequented gay clubs for the same reason). Although seven in thirty had given up 'dance drugs' (except cannabis) when I interviewed them, only one in thirty had given up the club and party lifestyle. It was definitely something to do with this:

It is curious that a drug which can increase emotional closeness, enhance receptivity to being sexual and would be chosen as a sexual enhancer, does not increase the desire to initiate sex
(BUFFUM AND MOSER, 1986)

An abundance of sexual and sensual feelings, but actually 'doing' sex had lost its pride of place in the new chemical Britain after dark. (Those who stayed at home and took Ecstasy for sex on a Friday night excepted.) And not just for girls. Many a boy lost the will (and the ability, in some cases) to get it up. Girls could behave in a way not always possible outside the club/party environment. Boys were no longer a sexual nuisance or threat:

> We were trying to find this rave in Ardwick in deserted flats somewhere. I remember me and [her female friend] being dumped by a cab in what felt like the middle of nowhere and seeing this gang of lads coming towards us. Luckily they were on 'E' so there was no problem.

They felt safe at clubs, parties and raves. Roving round on your own was part of the form, they knew where the crowd they went with were to be found. A friendly hello from a bloke didn't mean he would have his tongue down your throat before you could say, 'Shut Up and Dance'. Not a sexual partner but sensations of the 'Mind, Body or Soul' were what being 'Luvdup' was all about. Strangers gave them cigarettes, water, massages and generally looked out for them. They did the same for strangers. Perhaps this is why the girls I spoke to tended to rate recreational drug use above recreational or casual sex. Social and sexual relations on the dancefloor had been transformed. They were actors in a huge social and sensual landscape.

Auto-eroticism, no simple or boring narrative of hunting a sexual partner, flirtation without tears and messy knickers you hadn't planned on, camaraderie – it was too good to be true. Forget sinister men wanting and having their way with innocent girls with no mind of their own. At a time when the official world was beginning to panic about 'heterosexual AIDS', this was girly safer sex writ large! More imaginative than the leering moral outrage party could ever dream of. No innocent and frail young maidens duped by drug 'pushers' and falling victim to unstoppable male urges these. More like willing participants in a culture where gender still shapes the rules but being 'up-for-it' is the name of the game. Meet the modern girl, the female 'Me' of that Generation. Nurtured on another generation's bra-burning, weaned on *Cosmo* you-can-do-it and nourished on a diet of Maggie and Madonna.

BEYOND FEAR AND EASE

Old fashioned girls duped into a dangerous sex-and-drug fest or post-feminist babes, active and powerful participants in a limitless sensual and safer sex pleasure zone? You already know I'm going to say Just Say Think beyond these extremes.

SEX AND DRUGS AND ... ER, TECHNO

Number one. The picture of girly Ease I've painted was definitely the way they told it to me and the way it looked in the early nineties. And it was definitely a widespread female experience. But it wasn't the whole story then and it's by no means the whole story now – there's potentially more sex, more drugs and more danger now than ever. Yet the party still goes on.

I have to admit I was impressed when I interviewed girls from culturE. In fact, in many ways it seemed like a (post-) feminist dream. It looked like Ecstasy and house culture had provided the landscape, or catalyst even, for social change. Not only were opposing class, race, ethnic and other identity cultures at peace in this zone but the white flag seemed to be flying in the sex war too. Exploring your sexuality, identity, personal power; pleasuring yourself (and others); being social on a grand stage; having male (body) 'mates' had never been quite like this before for girls. Any history of youth culture could tell you that. From my own experience, being a hippy chic may have been one of the closest things to it but – let's face it – that 'one thing' was still so often what the (white) boys danced for. 'Free love' was often only hassle-free for the boys. But now girls had climbed off the back of scooters and into their own youth cultural driving seat for good.

The (female) liberating aspect of the culture clearly still survives in some quarters. Girls in 1996 still refer to the lack of 'copping off' pressure as a major part of the enjoyment they get out of the dance/party scene. But as the culture has diversified, mutated and regenerated over the years, it has become more sex'd up. Invading 'beer monsters' used to think they were on to a good thing with girl 'ravers' and find they got short shrift. The return of alcohol and the rise of cocaine in the culture seem to have accompanied a more gritty return to the 'FLESH'. Wearing the latest funky 'back to the future' outfit can get you ogled in just the way the girls in my study in the North West were bored with, depending on the club or party. Sex and drugs also seem to feature more in a girl's dream of hedonism. Girls are to be found out on sexual safari in many an urban night-time jungle, hunting men and moving in for the kill (Campbell, 1996). In the regular photographic round-up of the nation's clubbers, Mixmag asked 'What would you do with a million pounds?'. 'Victoria, care assistant', answered 'I'd get off me cake'. 'Nicola, in purchasing', replied, 'I'd spend it on sex, drugs and more sex' (Mixmag, 1993). If the Ecstasy honeymoon phase in Britain was all about polysensuality, things are now much more likely to get back to sexual basics.

The sexualization process was heralded as early as 1992, as earlier androgynous 'baggy', hippy and 'sunshine holiday' clothes styles gave way to, among many other styles which borrowed from the sporting world, tiny tops and hot pants for women or skimpy Lycra, then rubber, PVC and leather outfits.

The sexual temperature is definitely rising. Perhaps it's the recession, sex isn't exactly the preserve of the rich. Perhaps it's just old taboos and morals being beaten down. Perhaps not but there's no mistaking that sex is an increasingly prevalent subject ... Over in New York the clubs are having the biggest explosion of lust since the backroom bacchanalia from before AIDS hit the States ... these clubbers have been wise to AIDS since before they were having sex. But awareness of the virus doesn't seem to be stopping them.
MIXMAG, 1992

'Loved up or fucked up?' asked a feature on sex and drugs in the same issue. The style mag, i-D's November 1992 'Sexuality Issue', dubbed the 'sexiest magazine in the world', vaunted an 'A–Z of safe sex; new pornography, sexy fashion, queer fanzines, ragga dances and fetish wear' among other things. Many club nights used more sexually explicit names: 'Love To Be' in Sheffield offered 'Penetrating Saturdays, Deep into August'. This sexualization of club culture was part of a broader trend. The pages of *Cosmopolitan* had proclaimed, 'Give me dangerous sex' as early as 1990, in a knee-jerk response to 'the alleged New Puritanism' in the age of AIDS. 'The sexiness of sex must be kept alive though we walk in the shadow of death' was the maxim asserted as more closely fitting individual experience of sexuality in the eighties than 'lifestyle advertisements of designer condoms' suggested. It was a sign of the times. The retreat from AIDS nerves into a sexplosion had begun.

If there's more sex and drugs, it's more dangerous now too. Not in the tabloid melodrama way, with 'evil' men feeding girls drugs in order to have their way (although the older-more-powerful-man – DJ, promoter, etc – lording it over a young bit of stuff syndrome has not been blown out by the wind of Ecstasy). The business opportunities of a continually booming, if changing, culture have provided for all levels of the crime career structure – as drug dealing, security staff and club 'protection', etc, offer senior and junior positions, as well as out and out gang warfare. Once united youth tribes aren't always full of love and peace any more. Violence can be part of the landscape too. Take these two 20-something career girls' stories told to me in 1994:

> There was this programme on TV recently which showed this lad drunk and everything in a club and the bouncers were pretending to be so polite. Well I know for a fact that the bouncers there don't think twice about putting your head through a glass door! ... Some lad a few weeks ago in [a Manchester club] took two jackets off these lads, took some draw off them and the bouncers were just laughing at them. Another lad came out, just smashed one of these lads in the face, took all his money and went home – with the bouncers!

> We went to this rave in Ashton and it was a real mix – Salford lads and mad crusties. It really kicked off – people beating each other with sticks and anything they could get their hands on. People driving straight at people with cars. There must have been a lot of people half killed that night. People all covered with blood.

It wasn't as bad in the early nineties but girls I interviewed then talked about the shady characters to be increasingly found in clubs, while they described the sexual safety they felt. Then and now, all this acknowledged crime and danger makes little difference to the attraction and enjoyment for girls.

So why, in the Luvdup days before Ecstasy-fuelled chemical culture became really, really big business in the nineties, were the tabloid horror stories of the single white female's demise at the hand of dastardly men at their most sexy? Why the sexual threat of drugs? Two main creatures scuttle out from under the lid of this fear immediately: the threat of 'heterosexual AIDS' and a traditional reaction to a non-traditional thing – girls taking drugs publicly – in large numbers.

SEX AND DRUGS? SUITS YOU SIR

By autumn 1988, the British population was acquainted with the concept of 'heterosexual AIDS' (even if most still perceived the retrovirus as a predominantly gay or 'junky' problem). 'Heterosexual AIDS' first went public big time in early 1987 with the government's billboard and every-door-in-the-nation leaflet campaign, 'AIDS: Don't Die Of Ignorance'. 'Anyone can get it, gay or straight, male or female. Already 30,000 people are infected', ran the copy. 'At the moment the infection is mainly confined to relatively small groups of people in this country. But it is spreading', it continued. 'AIDS is not prejudiced. It can kill anyone', said another poster. And that wasn't all of it. By 1986, two years after HIV infection was first recorded among Edinburgh's injecting drug users, up to half of those tested were HIV positive. Between September 1987 and January 1988, the British government ran a public information campaign against drug use and AIDS. The moral fever was running high when news of youthful use of the 'love' drug, Ecstasy, first hit.

'Young people who frequent London's trendiest night clubs and use the new designer drug "Ecstasy" are returning to promiscuous sex despite warnings about the danger of AIDS', warned The Observer, on cue, as the drug service field, increasingly awash with public money to contain HIV infection among drug injectors, turned their attention to the new craze. 'We're worried about the new Acid House scene. The London club scene is a high risk area as there are close links between casual sex, drug abuse and AIDS', said the director of the Standing Conference on Drug Abuse (SCODA). To professionals with an eagle eye for risk, here was a new opportunity.

The link between recreational drug use, sex and HIV was already being made in America, as the sex lives of gay men were probed to investigate the connection between drug use and unsafe sex. (Stall et al, 1986; Stall, 1988). As moral outrage and castigation of all things gay mounted with the AIDS panic, a public happy to point the moral finger at other people's sex lives, got twitchy when the 'AIDS affects us all' doctrine took off big time, after (hetero)sexual transmission in others besides 'other' people in distant developing countries was discovered. For a moral panic involving a rogues gallery of 'deviant' sex, drugs and preying 'foreigners', a new youth cult involving a 'love' drug consumed in hedonistic environments would do very nicely as raw material thank you. The fact that 'Luvdup' did not necessarily mean 'sexdup', that Ecstasy's shrinking effects on male basic instincts, although by no means universal, were nonetheless contributing significantly to new, less genitally-orientated sexual codes in culturE – was lost in the moral maelstrom of retrovalues spawned by the HIV retrovirus.

SICK SLUT OR SILK CUT?: MAD, BAD AND DANGEROUS GIRLS

If the moral landscape of AIDS provided the contemporary backdrop to the new 'warped drug cult', the retrovalues surrounding women's drug use were good for a much longer historical one. Take the twenties, for example. Then the single white female starred in a different drama but on similar lines. This time she was duped by 'Chinamen' into smoking opium and taking cocaine to fuel her dancing at West End nightclubs. Once more a highly publicized, drug-induced death, that of the West End actress, Billie Carlton, had set the tone, her star status combining with her opium and cocaine use to provide a focus for such anxieties in 1918. The heady mix of drug use (cocaine and opium) with the supposedly malign influence of 'men of colour' and the 'frailty' of the women who associated with them became key components of the post-First World War popular imagination (Kohn, 1992).

The belief that the female of the species doesn't go in for mindchanging substances (or at least not in any way the same as the male) is well entrenched. Retro gender values which prescribe that nice girls 'just don't' are hard to budge. And it's not just the moral outrage party in the tabloid media which has kept the femininity-into-euphoria-abandon-generally-altered-states-doesn't-go equation going. Girls who 'do' have been portrayed as taking a route to the wrong side of the morality tracks by women's magazines, parents and male peers. The unattractiveness of this particular road to ruin for the female of the species is perpetuated by a largely gender-blind drugs research literature which mostly follows the exploits and attitudes of men. When women do gain the stage, it is as morally weaker, sicker and more addicted characters (unfit mothers, prostitutes, traditional in outlook and fresh out of self-esteem) – playing bit parts as victims to men's starring role as (sometimes) lovable rogues out on the margins. Utterly dependent, hooked on drugs by men and thereon in dependent on them for drugs and, often, to inject them – that's the dominant image of girls and drugs. Think of the girl in *Trainspotting* and you get the general idea.

But it's more than a trifle difficult to recognize culturE girls in this image. They aren't looked down on within the culture as abnormal; they are as likely to have got into drugs through a girlfriend as a boyfriend and are quite capable of buying their own. Drugs for them are part of a culture involving music, dancing, fashion, magazines – the high street, not the low-life. Like it or not, the modern girl was in 1988, and still is, tuning in, turning on, if not frequently dropping out. Figures put young women ahead in smoking tobacco and they're doing their fair share of notching up the units of alcohol too. The same studies which suggest that youthful chemical culture has hit bigger time than ever before in British post-war history, also suggest that young women are close to or level pegging with their male peers when it comes to taking LSD, cannabis, amphetamine and Ecstasy and even outstripping them in some cases. Supermodels get drug problems, tell the world ... and carry on working. Courtney Love admits she did drugs in an offhand way in *Vanity Fair* and Uma Thurman plays a gangster's moll nineties-style in *Pulp Fiction*, complete with illegit-Yuppie coke habit. She's no airhead. She's hip and, although she pays a price for her drug highs, this portrayal of female drug use is notably lacking in more usual invitations to morally condemn.

This seemingly new-found freedom to 'puff' as much and 'neck' as many 'E's, as much whizz or acid as the lads may be a debatable one. Especially when you see the same 'girly macho' which gets girls drinking pints applied to drugs. Especially when the girls doing it discover they can 'cane it' big time and keep it together better than the guys. But the times are definitely a-changing. It can seem like the mothers and carers of tomorrow, the future guardians of back-to-basics home and hearth morality, are shrugging off their responsibilities, donning the glad rags of many a yesteryear (all mixed up together at once) and giving themselves up to the hedonism of the end of the century party. No wonder the sex and drugs moral outrage party has set its sights on the single white female and the nation's parents are so worried about their daughters. But, questionable though the freedom to overdo drugs may be, let's not kid ourselves it's the drugs alone which get the moral high ground going. It's the fact that such a 'freedom' exists that's at the root of fear. That the girls are *not* innocent, passive creatures.

PENIS UNENVY, LADETTES AND LET-DOWNS: BABES IN OR OUT OF THE WOOD?

When I did the study on girls, sex and drugs in Manchester (1991–1993), I concluded that I had truly met the modern girl in the young women who came to my city centre office and my home

(Henderson, 1993a). Whether they did drugs or not, these young women were admirable in so many ways. In a context of recession and diminishing opportunities in education and job markets, the self-confidence, the drive and keenness to get on (either outside or inside the official world), the capacity for pleasure in their own physicality, the commonsense of these young women (most of them not from privileged backgrounds) was wonderful to behold. Compared to a much larger study of young women's sexuality friends and colleagues of mine had recently conducted in London and Manchester, these girls were so sexually confident, knew what they wanted, dressed for their own pleasure, weren't pathetic creatures whose sexual pleasure was non-existent or totally buried under their boyfriend's requirements (Holland et al, 1990).

The fact that over half of them lived with friends or on their own and a third still lived with their family suggested that the old female story of romance, marriage and the kitchen sink was clearly of limited attraction as the option for the future. 'Finding Mr Right' did feature among the dreams and aspirations of some but they all, whether unemployed, working or in full-time education, often dreamed of foreign holidays, travelling abroad and having a good job. Against a wider background where the future may have become an uncertain concept for many generations and living for the moment a more general pursuit, the longer term clearly mattered to these young women in terms of achieving personal fulfilment in a range of social spheres. I felt so strongly that both the drugs research literature and much feminist analysis of modern femininity (and masculinity) had got it wrong, I gave conference papers and wrote a couple of articles to argue my case (Henderson, 1993b; c; and d). The idea was to stimulate debate – instead it got (a few) other women's backs up and a flurry of letter writing followed.

But things have changed since then. I'm not so certain as I was. For starters, I've recognized I was pushing things to make a strategic point. For another thing, the honeymoon days of Ecstasy use are well over and it's easier to see its dark side – the ill effects of the drug itself and the changes for the worse within the culture – around gender, among many other things. But that doesn't mean I'm going back to basics on the girls, drugs and sex front, and joining the media in stalking the single white female. I just think it's more complicated. We're talking about, among many other things, femininity (and masculinity) currently up for grabs.

In many ways the identity of the modern girl I discovered being forged in house clubs, warehouses, fields up and down the land was, and has gone further, mainstream. It's been very notable in the women's magazine world since *Cosmo* heralded the post-AIDS fear sexplosion back in 1990. It's common understanding these days that these magazines push both sex and a 'gagging for it', 'can do it' female sexual identity in a big way. Once debate raged about Madonna, pop sextress extraordinaire, with many (among the chattering classes) arguing hers is a 'sexual-physical pleasure that has nothing to do with men' (Fiske, 1989). Now fetish and bondage clothing, body piercing and tattoos, fantasies, once confined to gay and punk subculture and speciality sex clubs, are now part of the mainstream. Even the boy pin-up diet of adolescent girls in the nineties includes healthy portions of what used to be gay soft porn. The TV programme *Eurotrash*, with the interplay between its gay and straight front men, illustrates better than most the 'post-modern' ironic ethic around sex in youth culture.

And women seem to be getting their share of the fun. Body-conscious girls yenjoy themselves en masse in Japan. Club 18–30 advertises by inviting them to 'Discover your erogenous zones', in 'Beaver Espana', in a 'Summer of 69'. The 'Girls – Can we interest you in a package holiday?' ad shows a well-padded pair of boxer shorts. Cute, figure hugging T-shirts proclaim 'Hot and Horny', 'This Bitch Fights Back', 'Babe Power', 'Dolly Bird', 'Friction Sista', 'Nice Tits',

'Kiss My Ass', 'Love It' – among many other things – in an ironic
send-up of all things sexist and all things anti-sexist. 'Why do you go
clubbing?' asked the May 1993 edition of Mixmag, in its customary
photographic round-up of the nation's clubbers. 'Why? To look for
photographers' answers one young woman. 'Why? I go to perform'
says another. 'Why? The drugs are crap at home' says yet another. All
challenge the camera with a great deal of bare flesh, self-contained
expressions and very large eye pupils. A month earlier, the same
magazine asked 'Who do you love?'. 'Who? Me', replies a female
London banker at a night called 'Orgasm'. 'Who? My washing
machine. It vibrates. And this photo better get me a shag', replies a
female aerobics teacher at 'Cream' in Liverpool. 'Who? Everyone',
answers an unemployed young woman at 'Betty Ford Clinic'. The
'Ministry of Sound's 1995 Sex Survey of the bedtime habits of (4,000)
British clubbers found that 31 per cent of female clubbers had had
group sex and 61 per cent of clubbers had had sex in a public place. It
also found that 94 per cent of men and 79 per cent of women were
seriously condom-conscious with a new partner (Mixmag, 1996b). Now
there's even virtual sex in cyberspace. Hey, welcome to the quirky,
ironic nineties. It's sexy fun all the way to the end of the century.

Acting outrageous, striking a pose, putting your body out. I'm the
first one to love the humour and irony of it all, the power of today's
'babes with attitude' to put two fingers up to it all and get on with
their lives. You want to strut your stuff in white trash tack, mixed
with seventies black power, throw in a bit of fifties secretary or
housewife, a touch of forties movie star perhaps? Fine. A dollop of
hippy chic maybe? Tribal trinkets? Or perhaps a smidgeon of space
couture? Push-up ultra-bra? Squash-'em flat bodice? Brilliant, from
where I stand. Just Say Pussy Power. Which is nice. But it's not all
good news. And some of it isn't news at all. When the Wonderbra first
said 'Hello Boys', I was still arguing irony and post-modern fun. But
the media birth of the ladette and the new lass was harder to

swallow. In fact, I really didn't like the taste. After all the hype, the snarling up-yours-boys, we're-having-a-chat-and-a-giggle girlies on late-night TV were not only not very funny, witty or clever, it was hard to spend your time *not* looking down their cleavage. Is this what we really want? Sexual confidence is all well and good (in fact it's brilliant!), especially if you have the power to just say no to sex and to body consciousness, if you choose. Tits and bums are great Carry On fun but recently cleavages seem to be everywhere you look. Suddenly the irony seems to have gone flat. It seems to me that they've crossed too far over the thin line, and I know I'm not alone. Suddenly, post-feminist icons look suspiciously like boring old sexploitation.

Living up to images of modern femininity is a bit of a tall order. The post-modern Ms is not necessarily 'gagging for it' and full of poise, confidence and wit *all* of the time, far from it. Ask Sara Cook, the 13-year-old Essex girl who couldn't wait to run off to Turkey, get married and be an old fashioned girl (albeit in an 'exotic' way). On the doing-sex-with-men front, as J.K. Collins (*For Women* agony aunt and sexpert with a sense of humour and more than the usual touch of girl-friendliness) has pointed out in her recent book, 'Sex does appear to be growing more "women friendly" – but it remains in something of a foreplay stage' (Collins, 1996). Most sexpertise, still the mainstay of many women's and sex magazines alike, still casts women in the role of a 'please your man' heterosexuality. And girls who go for it are getting turned down by men – who don't like their women too sexually confident.

Sexual confidence is also all well and good if you've got some other tangible power in the world too. The two often go together, it is true, but where else is babe power these days, apart from in their 'attitude'? In these 'post-feminist' times, women aren't immune from a raw deal at work, in the pocket, at home, in politics and, even, in the media. Meanwhile, society has little to offer so many among the young. No wonder some are saying Just Say No to all the female rules.

One day bra wars, the next gang wars. Girls just want to have guns, we are told, as much as the boys. They too are mean and violent. Ask the man who saved actress Liz Hurley 'from 4 Burly Girlies', as the press described the girls who robbed her in the street in November 1994. Even the girls who tried to take themselves out of the consumer world appear in cartoon form as Tank Girl. Girls behaving badly isn't just a media invention, they've done it since time began, but this kind of power mongering is more than a little worrying. What kind of freedom is freedom to do as many drugs, as much sex and crime as the boys?

Back to the twenties, another time when the single white female, the modern girl (or 'flapper') featured in public debate and pop iconography. She too was hedonistic and independent. Her drugtaking and sexual vulnerability also featured in the popular media drug story. Sex sells. And sex has always been the favourite for portraying deviance in female form. The twenties version of the drugtaking single white female figured prominently in the popular portrayal of post-war anxieties surrounding the enormous economic independence and social emancipation gained by women during the First World War. In the nineties, she's figuring again – as a major transformation in the economic bases and political make-up of countries across the globe has, along with feminism, made for a changing shape to femininity.

Why single and why white, is more than a little uncomfortable to answer. Why single is easy. Only singles are threatening to the old order because they aren't 'properly' protected, i.e. by a man. But why white? Surely it can't be that the moral outrage party doesn't feel the need to protect the non-white daughters of Britain? Femininity is still on the change but at the moment it's all up for grabs. None of us really knows if 'the chance to stand up for what you want', for the 'sisters' is just an advert for Ryvita (which tells us that wanting crispy bacon, fried tomatoes, a dripping free-range egg and demanding real food values, in the shape of Ryvita, is a freedom worth standing up for) or the final rallying call before all is finally different but equal in the sex and gender landscape.

Just Say Watch This Space. (And realize there's more to the drug Ecstasy than meets the public eye.)

6

Chemical culture
and modern manhood

Of course, there's another side to the genderscape in the Ecstasy case. Looking at how the modern girl has been shaping up in nineties chemical Britain after dark and in the adult world's interpretation of her, is to see only half the picture. So what do we see if we pursue my line of inquiry and look *at* and then beyond the popular certainties about the modern boy? You can bet that, whatever it is, it won't be case solved. Let's begin with the side of the generational divide that sees only fear when it looks at culturE.

FEAR

As we've already begun to discover, if the changing face of the single white female has played a leading victim role in the drugs melodrama, the male lead has been cast in the role of the evil perpetrator of crime – source of the drugs, the music and the venues for dance events. The culprit responsible for it all. Where she is all innocence, he is full of blame.

MR BIGS, SADISTIC PSYCHOS AND PLIERS OF DEADLY WARES

We could hardly believe it … We have seen drug pushers before but nobody quite like this. He was wearing a pinstripe suit as he walked around handing out his leaflets. He was about 45 to 50 and had receding hair. Everybody thought he stuck out like a sore thumb but he just carried on … He said he didn't have the drug on him but … he would come back later if people wanted any.

SOUTH WALES ECHO (HORTON, 1986)

Unlike the pretty young image of his female counterpart, our male lead has been played by a more diverse range of social groups. One of his earliest faces marked him out as different from previous drug dealers, more an old style businessman, but complete with eighties-style product-brochure marketing technique (immediately cast as one of his evil calling cards). When Acid House hit the nation's breakfast tables in autumn 1988, this evil businessman image was given more detail and a sharper eighties edge. The 'Mr Bigs' of Acid House were cast as evil versions of that emblem of Britain in the eighties, the Yuppie. White, male and middle class and into all things 'designer', from watches, to living accommodation and … mobile phones. Even the most 'evil' and 'deadly' of his 'wares', Ecstasy, was ascribed a 'designer' label (although this later became, inaccurately, confused with the pharmaceutical process of 'designing' or altering the molecular structure of scheduled drugs to avoid prosecution while maintaining their psychoactive properties).

The initial 'Mr Bigs' were party organizers but, by implication or outright accusation, also drug dealers. Organizers portrayed like

'Smug', 'Wheeler Dealer' Roger Goodman, or 'Mr Ecstasy', pictured in his Soho office, 'headquarters of his sinister Acid House drugs operation', in a piece which 'exposed' him, in December 1988, as 'the evil drug baron behind the Acid House party craze'. A 'squat 29 year old', 'from a wealthy London family', this 'utter menace' was accused by The People of supplying drugs not only to pop stars but also to parties attended by 'up to 4,000 teenagers at a time, each paying £10 for admission to the midnight-to-dawn bashes as well as £1 for a glass of fizzy lemonade' (The People, 1988).

> Sadistic psycho ... spread a web of drugs terror across Scotland. [He] was caged for 17 years after a drug deal went wrong. And today the Sunday Mail can reveal the face of the criminal Tsar ... and how his evil empire of drugs, kidnapping, torture and mutilation netted him millions.
>
> (SILVESTER, 1996)

However, the image of the male lead changed over the years which saw the dance music scene diversify but increase its hold on the cultural mainstream and, with it, the demand for drugs. For starters, the image didn't stay middle class although, where specific reference to Ecstasy dealing was concerned, it remained largely white. (And the mobile phone, downgraded from its eighties Yuppie image in the nineties, became a major prop.) Even in 1988, an 'East End "firm" of gangsters' was said to have threatened to break 'Dodgy Roger, The Acid House King's legs after being double-crossed in a drugs deal'. The 'drug gang', already well established in the public mind via other drug sagas, such as the crack scare, and the horror stories which were media coverage of international drug trafficking, also stepped into the Ecstasy arena. A 1996 version of the Kray-type image of East End gangland featured in the aftermath of Leah Betts' death. The 'psycho' allegedly responsible for the 'web of drugs across Scotland', was also none other than the 'demon barber of Basildon',

CHEMICAL CULTURE AND MODERN MANHOOD

resident of 'Essex Badlands', 'the old East End by the sea', 'the north Thames corridor down which the drug dealers rat-run from Holland to Harwich to Southend-on-Sea to Tilbury'. Jailed for 17 years for a range of offences, including conspiracy to supply drugs, and grievous and actual bodily harm, this 'Ecstasy baron' was also held responsible, by insinuation, for the 'barbarism behind "murder" ' of Leah Betts, 'barbarism' involving tales of torture and death among the drug gangs of Essex (Sweeney, 1996).

But, just as the initial older-world 'pinstripe' image gave way to 'evil' Yuppiedom, these 'psychos' from gangland were also new kids on the block, outnumbering the older 'gentlemen' from the East End, who had lost their codes and taboos around drug taking and dealing and honed in on a new business opportunity, often spotted while 'doing time' (i.e. witnessing the wide availability of drugs in prison). Here was a new version of organized crime altogether. Younger, playing for higher, instant wealth stakes with none of the codes or taboos of their predecessors and no sense of 'working their way up' the criminal career structure:

A lot of younger guys ... didn't come up the way the older criminal did, by being a thief or fence or whatever. Now all of a sudden, they're buying three or four thousand Ecstasy pills in Holland and ... making bundles of money. They're millionaires at 23.
SPANISH-BASED BRITISH DRUG SMUGGLER, DEREK MAUGHAN
(QUOTED IN CAMPBELL, 1994)

These reworked Krays weren't the only perpetrators of the new drug evil. The nineties saw a diversification of dealing networks all the way down the chain and new 'young upstarts' were to be found at all levels. The growing culturE offered a thriving illicit wealth creation scheme to lads up for just a little or a lot of ducking and diving. Going solo to supplement your own drug use, welfare benefits or a college grant was also an option – although steering clear of the territories claimed by the ruling gangs could be a problem. 'I sold 'E's at coma girl's club' revealed the *Daily Mirror*, as hopes faded for Leah Betts, lying in a coma after taking Ecstasy at her 18th birthday party (Edwards and Midgley, 1995). 'Whoever sold that pill knew they were selling her poison. The pushers don't give a damn', the unidentified man told us, as he described how dealers 'laced' their wares with rat killer, toilet cleaner, guitar wax and a sealing coat of hairspray.

But whatever their status in the illicit world of Ecstasy dealing, the evil nature of these men has been established in a remarkably similar fashion over the years. Dovetailing neatly with the purveyors of all illegal drugs, the image has been of ruthless men who will stop at nothing for money. Amoral and totally unmoved by the devastation they cause, they knowingly entice the young with their deadly wares. As party organizer, drug dealer and producer of the 'killer music', the pipe which, in the popular version of the early days of Acid House on the grown-up side of the generational divide, led the young innocents to meet their doom, the male of the species is culprit number one in the Ecstasy case.

EASE

SHUT UP AND DANCE: BIG TIME SENSUALITY ON THE 'E' HONEYMOON: II

Needless to say, it's a very different kettle of fish when viewed from the other side of the lifestyle gap. The drug and the culture that offered the modern girl a landscape of sociability and sensuality she could explore as a relatively free agent, was that way because of changes in the boys too. Forget venturing onto the dancefloor at midnight to shuffle drunkenly about with the night's catch, forget dance techniques and skill displays, in 'the Summer of Love' of 1988 and for a few years to come, group feeling, sensation, letting go and non-verbal communication were all-inclusive. Forget social difference too – black/white, gay/straight, whatever class – the boys were far from a sinister threat, they were all Luvdup along with the girls.

> Old Manchester. Raincoats. Gloom. Misery ... In less than a month, the Hacienda was transformed from a 'cool' fridge that 'chilled' in too many ways, to a crazy party zone ... one day ('Happy Mondays') Shaun and Bez motored back from London with a boot full of peace 'n' love ... And Manchester discovered drugs; the students were away; pupils dilated, 2,000 batty clubbers danced like flower pot men; podiums were scaled and bubbles blown ... The city partied. One nation under a groove.
>
> CHAMPION, 1990

The in-depth study of culturE I was funded to conduct looked at girls, so I can't offer you the boys' version of Ease straight from the horse's mouth in the same way. But I can piece it together. And I'll start with the lads I got to know/know more about through their female peers, through friends and colleagues – the young residents of Manchester, one section of whom, possibly, gave culturE its most white working-class male public image.

Picture if you will a male culture of boozing, shagging and football ... violence. A fiercely heterosexual world far away from the PC politeness of caring men in touch with their emotions, their female partner's G-spot, her kitchen sink and their offspring; from men in touch with the emotions of other men enough to 'share' their feelings in a discussion group. A world where, instead, the sex war is a bloodier, more in-yer-face affair altogether. A male culture where identity at its strongest revolves around the mass gathering of football (before it went trendy), complete with roaring crowds, horns, whistles, the feeling of social belonging and ... the rush of beating men from the other side to a pulp. Never adverse to the city after dark, this culture stumbles upon a nocturnal landscape with a difference. One with a drug – which cuts your inhibitions, your desire to fight *and* your genital-fixation down to size – at its heart. Picture this same male culture becoming part of a heaving mass of bodies, roaring, blowing horns and whistles, letting the music take control, exploring a way of physical being they'd never allowed before ... and loving it. Embracing strangers, whoever they are, smiling at them instead of groping them or ramming a beer glass in their face. A somewhat girly way of being viewed from gritty macho mountain, all hugs, massages and flirting with no testosterone. This was a dance culture which in fact, 'saw many males, lads of Madchester included, regress to an adolescent sexual state' (Carroll, 1992).

Of course this particular male culture was only one of many drawn into culturE. And a lot of the lads I've come into contact with have little in common with this version of masculinity. As with the modern girl, many a modern boy I've met has left me feeling optimistic about the genderscape of the future, was a pleasure to meet. But the fact that even this extreme end of boydom went all Luvdup on the dancefloor illustrates a wider point. Something was happening to the nation's lads after dark. Like the girls I interviewed in Manchester told me at the time – about both the men who 'belonged' to the scene and the men who didn't:

Lads dance a lot more than they would at other clubs and it seems there's a lot more boys and girls together rather than boys at one side of the dance floor and girls in the middle. Lads will come up and talk to you more – but often the last thing on their mind is getting off with you.

You see lots of lads hugging each other, a lot ... Sometimes they hug for so long you think 'When's the big snog coming?'

Younger (gay) guys are going straight onto the rave scene and leaving the high energy scene ... It's taken the seriousness out of it for a lot of boys I know. A lot of them feel ... a lot less worried about being cruised by a man while they're out. Going out for a good time rather than just to cop off. It's totally changed the scene, split it in a lot of ways.

When I was at this private rave, I'd just come up on my 'E' and two guys came in. I'd say they were perhaps about 35, and at first we thought they were undercover cops. And everybody knew what everybody else was thinking and everybody was staring at them because they weren't dancing normally. They were, like, shaking about, like, being really stupid like they were pissed. And everybody started moving away from them, you know?

You can always spot them, men who think 'let's go to one of these here raves' and 'these girls are probably goers'. They stand there with pints of beer and ask you if you come here often.

Like Irvine Welsh, acclaimed Scottish writer on the new chemical culture, tells it in his book, *Marabou Stork Nightmares*, his soccer-casual lead character's description of his personal culturE make-over in Manchester captures the general experience well:

A lot of the boys in the cashies took 'E's, a lot of them didnae. I never saw the point. I'd always liked the Becks, and couldna get intae that fucking music. It was shite, that techno, nae lyrics tae it, that same fuckin drum machine, throbbin away aw the time. I hated dancing ...

I was lost in the music and the movement. It was an incredible experience, beyond anything I'd ever known. I could never dance but all self-consciousness left me as the drug and the music put me in touch with an undiscovered part of myself ... My body's internal rhythms were pounding, I could hear them for the first time. They were singing: You're alright, Roy Strang ... People, strangers, were coming up to me and hugging me. Birds, nice-looking lassies n that. Guys n aw; some ay them cunts that looked wide and whom I would have just panelled before ... Something special was happening and we were all in this together.
WELSH, 1995

Like a student dissertation (one of an explosion in student writing on culturE) told it, in an attempt to put into words a highly non-verbal individual experience and social event from a male perspective:

When you are on Ecstasy you can quite happily spend the whole night hugging, stroking, smiling together, acknowledging the people around you, and saying very little ... ideas of actually having sex do not arise until after the rave (where the need for sleep usually quenches the desire for sex).

When someone is on Ecstasy, that person ... will be continually confirming that those around them are feeling the same way. This involves much eye contact and smiling which maintains the group feeling of euphoria ... There is a need to keep checking that everyone around is 'still up there' which creates a close-knit pattern of interaction on the dancefloor ... the style of dancing is a response to the particular track being played.
CREED, 1993

Picture all this and you can begin to grasp the kind of make-over culturE gave modern manhood in Manchester. And in some ways, although its natives and social scientists alike may disagree,

Manchester has been like many a British city, or indeed country field, when it comes this shift in the nocturnal genderscape. If (probably) one of the most resistant to all things liberal and feminist versions of boydom could get all Luvdup – alongside students and legit-career boys weaned on another generation's feminism (if not through the family or college, then girlfriends' *Cosmo*), and out and proud gay boys, all from any part of the country or any ethnic origin – then surely culturE was really reaching the gender parts no other youth culture had quite done before?

BOYS STAY HOME AND COOK TUNES

And it didn't end at the dancefloor. The impact of the music, or derivations, which now soundtracks everything from football to holiday programmes to children's TV should not be underestimated. 'The music is the drug' was and is a motto central to house/dance cultures and not only their consumers. Dancing and driving to house music were one thing but it also democratized the music creation business like no other – as one man and his technology took over from the live music venue as a central feature of pop culture. All over the land, boys went to the bedroom or garage with a pile of vinyl (fetishized in the age of CDs, audio tapes and digital technology), a bag of cannabis, two turntables, a mixer, a sampler and some good friends – and had dancefloor and chart hits. Suddenly many a boy's fantasy was not to be a rock star complete with wailing guitar and mirror-formed pose, but the man who (facelessly and silently) orchestrates the moods and emotions of the dance crowds.

[Dancing] styles shift as the tunes change, and so the DJ has a degree of control over the action on the dancefloor. For instance, he can bring the dancers into a 'trance' state by playing a strong, repetitive, rhythmic track which turns the dancer's consciousness inwards – and then 'release' them by

'dropping' a well-known vocal track, at which point people are intensely
aware of those around them, creating an overall 'crescendo of emotion'
when people raise their hands, hug, and beam from ear to ear.
CREED, 1993

Once feminist academics filled the gender gap in stories about
youth cultures past (which were all male angst and girly passivity) by
writing about the private domestic world of girl 'teenybopper'
bedroom culture – all pop pin-ups and beauty tips. Now it was the
lads' turn to take over this girly space in pop culture. And while there
was plenty of 'trainspotting' ladism there for the taking in the
techniques, technology and terminology involved, this creative form
also became an emotional language for young men in a world on the
turn. They didn't stop at tuning into and turning on the emotional
state and mood of those listening in at many an evening at home or
at clubs and parties. Planning and composing tapes of non-stop tunes
raided from almost every type of music you can think of, became a
kind of emotional currency. A form of cultural exchange. Something
to give to those you were close to, those on the same 'vibe', and a
form of social identity, as well as being a new creative form. Like
Irvine Welsh said:

House culture is ... about individual spirituality, about attempting to
understand the entire psychic terrain an individual operates in. It'll never be
recognised as such ... the media and arts establishments could never bring
themselves to concede that an 18 year old unemployed person with a set of
decks and some good friends might be far more adept and advanced in the
whole life process of exploring their social and spiritual identity than they
could ever be.
WELSH, 1996B

CHEMICAL CULTURE AND MODERN MANHOOD

Forget men behaving badly, house music and drugs had stepped in and taken over where feminism had failed. It was male liberation like no other.

INTO UNCERTAINTY

Heinous villains or touchy, feely men in touch with themselves like never before? Let me be your guide beyond these opposing certainties.

RUFF ENUFF? IT'S A MAN'S, MAN'S WORLD

First of all, of course, the moral high ground haven't got it all wrong when they put crime and boyhood together. Official statistics have it that the male of the species commits the lion's share of indictable offences, violent crimes and burglaries in the UK. Meanwhile, the first-ever official study of youth crime based on interviews and not police figures (which do not record undetected crime), found that, between the ages of 14 and 17 years, girls are nearly as likely to be involved in offending as boys. At 14 to 17 years of age, 24 per cent of boys and 19 per cent of girls have committed at least one crime other than drug use or a driving offence. But girls are much more likely to grow out of crime: for boys aged 22 to 25 years, this figure rises to 31 per cent; for girls it drops to 4 per cent (although drug use continues at a high level for both) (Graham and Bowling, 1996).

They've also got a point when they identify the dark side of culturE with masculinity. Certain varieties of the male of the species do seem to have a firm hold on all things illicit in culturE. For instance, the supply of drugs; the organization of illegal raves and parties; the 'protection' of club owners and 'house' dealers; the violence and theft at nocturnal events; and the supply of security staff with no National Insurance number. Or put another way, the side of culturE which revolves around an illicit form of entrepreneurialism, a cash economy and a currency of violence.

But it's much less certain where the blame for all this lies than the official world allows. It's hard to stop being certain, especially if you've ever had (at the very least) your car stereo, TV or video nabbed (and nabbed again and again); especially if you live in a street or part of Britain where you're afraid for yourself and/or your kids because drug dealers are openly plying their trade and ploughing down their rivals on your doorstep (like parents and kids I've been interviewing lately); especially if you've been beaten to a pulp or been 'taxed' at a club lately. Watching your back is an everyday reflex in much of Britain these days and drugs are behind a lot of what we watch out for. But let's give being uncertain a try.

ARRESTED DEVELOPMENT? DRUGS, CRIME AND PERPETUAL ADOLESCENCE

Let me return to our Manchester love thug. He illustrates something rather more than how much the Ecstasy honeymoon affected boyhood on the dancefloor. After all, he's also a key example of what British politicians have been hot under the collar about for so long. The subject of much macho 'get tough on crime'-speak. The target of policy designed to put a stop to his criminal ways. American-style boot camps and 'zero-tolerance' policing strategies are recent proposals in a long line of measures to stem 'yob culture'.

Publicly prominent examples of this Manchester bad boy in the early days of culturE were the first band to emerge out of the ranks of the 'rave culture', the Happy Mondays. Dubbed 'Thatcher's illegitimate children' and credited with having 'put the "E" in Manchester', these 'arrogant, obnoxious and self-confessed "ugly cunts" ', 'just a bunch of dragged-up, drug-taking, badly dressed nutters' publicly exemplified a north Manchester-brand of 'Pills, Thrills 'n' Bellyaches' lifestyle in which 'blags' or 'scams' and hedonism are a way of life. 'Look, we play music in our spare time when we've got nothing else to do. The rest of it is one big fucking blag', singer Shaun Ryder told *NME* music magazine in characteristic style. But Manchester blag culture, of which the Happy Mondays were a public face, is only one of many versions of illicit ducking and diving in Britain in the nineties.

The Home Office study on youth crime identified a new class of career criminal involving nearly a third of young men. It warned that, for the first time, there is a generation of young men who are no longer 'growing out of crime' by their late teens, of 'perpetual adolescents' embedded in a criminal lifestyle fuelled by heavy use of alcohol and drugs. Challenging the government's dismissal of a link between crime and joblessness, the report pointed to youth unemployment as a contributing factor. But there was more: while girls mostly 'grow out of' crime by making the traditional transition from immature adolescent to mature adult, boys are less likely to do the things by which this transition is gauged – leaving school, leaving home, gaining economic independence, forming stable relationships, creating new families. And even if they do, they are still less likely to grow out of crime (Graham and Bowling, 1996). Basically, one of my colleagues doesn't seem far off the mark when he says:

> We have a very British underclass. They are the people who would have been the working class if there were any jobs left ... However, classifications are misleading not least because they mask or hide a large group of young people who are Thatcher's children in the sense that they believe in Thatcherite values of self-help and self-reliance. They want all the things they have been taught they should want. They are members of Britain's Scam Culture.
> GILMAN, 1993

ECSTASY: CASE UNSOLVED

Neither did i-D magazine's 1993 'Survival Issue':

Britain: a country on the blag? We all know someone who's on the blag.
Claiming dole whilst working cash-in-hand, selling knock-off gear – or
worse. In the midst of a recession, with Income Support at an all-time low,
we survey the state of the blag economy and ask, is scamming the last
great British industry?
EIMER, 1993

Now the last thing these lads give a fig about is if we rationally
try to explain their existence, put it down to 'society', take pity or just
carry on with bluster and the big lock-up. Many of them inhabit a
world where the official rules are surplus to requirements. They whirl
the rules. I didn't go interviewing 'young folk' in north Manchester
and Salford to not know that. But there is no way you can leave the
huge social changes in Britain over the last couple of decades out of
the equation. Left in many ways high and dry in, what Will Hutton
has called, a '40-30-30 society' (where 40 per cent have secure jobs, 30
per cent are in insecure part-time or contract work and 30 per cent
have no job at all), many among the young male of the species got on
their blagging bike and found a way of life. And culturE has provided
a rich seam of opportunity.

BOYS OWN

Opportunity not just of the illicit kind. The moral outrage party
again wasn't barking up entirely the wrong tree when it held lads
responsible for culturE. It's just that the boys have been highly creative
and productive. Much of the production, as opposed to consumption,
of the hydra-like dance cultures of modern Britain, *has* been in the lads'
hands. They *have* been central players in these new areas of cultural
industry – as DJs, promoters, magazine editors and contributors, etc.

Whoever it was brought house music and Ecstasy together is a total genius and I want to shake that man's hand.
ANONYMOUS (THE FACE, 1991)

Take the DJ. The most high profile figure in the 'faceless technology-based movement that is house'.

It seems more than a little odd, don't you think, that so many of pop music's biggest international earners and out-there innovators are women ... yet Britain's cooler-than-thou dance underground still appears to be, almost exclusively, a boys own club? ... Has house music's spirit of an open welcome, irrespective of race, sex or sexuality, really made inroads beyond the stroboscopic haze of the dancefloor? Are the nation's women really caught in the grip of techno-angst, or are they in fact itching to fiddle with the boys' equipment?
THOMPSON, 1994

A small but growing number of female DJs tell it like it is:
'I think a lot of women are scared off by the fact that when you DJ you know everyone's gonna be looking at you' explains 'Smokin' Jo', DJ of the month in May's *i-D* 1992 (Harpin, 1992) – a woman who 'has not let the fact that she remains one of the few black women DJs around worry her'. 'I'd hoped that rock and roll and the sexism that goes with it was dead. Maybe not, eh chaps? Let women into house music and judge us exactly as you'd judge men. No favouritism, no discrimination please!' challenges Pippa, one of two female DJs in Nottingham's DiY sound system (*DJ*, 1994). 'It's a load of bloody bollox isn't it? Music is fucking entertainment, just fucking music. I can't stand those boys who analyse it. Why intellectualise it? Music should have an immediate impact on the body, it's not the kind of thing where you should sit and think ...' screams Rachel Auburn, 'the peroxide thatched queen of

handbag house'. Her approach? 'DJing isn't so much a way of life as it is an excuse for a bloody good laugh. Delusions of grandeur are thrown strictly in the bin marked boring' (Generator, 1994). 'Just who is Mrs Woods?' asks *apn* magazine and informs its readers that 'in the Technotrash DJ stakes, the most high profile member of this elite body is a 40-year-old ex-Barnsley housewife'. (Hudson, 1994).

But although this cultural hero is mostly male, it's not a straightforward version of traditional masculinity. He may massage his ego with an entourage of hangers-on, many of whom will be admirers whose bodies replace the mixing decks after hours. He may be part of an exclusive and competitive boys' own club, bask in the god-like status he's often awarded, even. But that's not the end of the story. Above all else, he is renowned and faithfully followed for skills in mixing music into a continuous musical experience and an ability to tap into what the crowd are feeling. No longer the chattering 'personality' of yesteryear, the DJ in the box is a minister of emotional social affairs, an orchestrator of individual and communal mood.

HARDCORE, YOU KNOW THE SCORE?

This is where we part company with popular fear altogether. All this male emotional communication and taking the balls out of (male) sexuality just doesn't figure in the iconography of fear at all. But having looked beyond the 'E' honeymoon version of ladhood – where even football hooligans went all Luvdup and fluffy – we've begun to see there's a lot more to the Ease story too. And it doesn't end with the legal and illegal career opportunities culturE gave the lads either. The combination of music, Ecstasy and movement had an enormous effect on the genderscape in Britain after dark, offered some great opportunities for more than a little change. But not all the boys wanted it or were up to it. It may have blasted male bodily pleasure and identity away from the narrow and rigid base of 'that one thing', doing sex, at the time, and may still do it for some but it hasn't been the case for all blokes. 'Mr Wonderful' (captured in a cartoon-style leaflet by the Lifeline Project in Manchester) found new ways of getting what he wanted from the dancefloor in culturE:

> A friend of mine, Ben, thinks the worst thing about sex on drugs is not getting any. Ben says to tell you: Sex on drugs is fantastic and, according to him, Ecstasy is the best of the lot. 'My idea of a nightmare evening,' he says, 'is dropping an 'E' in a club when you're with your mates who have all got girlfriends. You start doing your mad 'E' dance in front of some girl, then, just after you've bought her a bottle of Evian, her boyfriend appears. By three o'clock in the morning you feel like taking your dick and putting it in the basebin.'
>
> MIXMAG, 1992

And not all boys loosened up enough to go further with each other than shaking a hand or a friendly nod, especially with strangers. Like the girls in Manchester I interviewed had clocked, some boys were too afraid of being labelled gay.

> Girls don't bother as much about being classed as a lesbian, you know what I mean. It's not a big deal is it? I mean I go and hug my best mate. In a pub, you know what I mean, give each other a hug or we could walk in holding hands. It doesn't bother me that at all but I think lads have got more of a hang-up about it.

And it didn't stop there. As the pills and thrills in culturE diversified, some of those who had taken off into a more girly realm of huggy sensuality got more than a bit uncomfortable. Although the boys owned most of the house culture structure, things girly were dictating more in the nocturnal land of hugs and happiness of the mind, body and soul than you'd think.

First there was the relationship between the mainstream and the underground. Like I said before, it has been crucial to the longevity and growth of house/dance cultures in Britain. As culturE tightens its grip on the mainstream, so the underground defines itself against it and moves on. And so the party continues. When 'Techno Tracy' became a vogue way of deriding 'plastic' as opposed to 'authentic' ravers in the early nineties, it was very telling. Viewed from the butch 'hardcore' underground, the mainstream is femme – all froth and no substance.

Then there was the whole Luvdup ethic – how girly and fluffy can you get? But there was something else. It was the girly 'E' types themselves: 'Upfront, bold and loud, they've learnt how to party and how to put a distance between flirting and fucking' (Marcus and Eshan, 1991). The ones who, in the words of more than one of my female interviewees 'gave out more' in this social setting. The ones Irvine Welsh's lad character, Ally, in 'An Acid House Romance' calls 'Hiya Lassies' and 'Sexy Feminists'.

> Party Chicks, Straight-Pegs, Skankers or Hounds, that's the four types ay bird ... Maistly Party Chicks in here, thank fuck ... Hiya Lassies are called so because they always say hi-ya-uh ... when they meet you ... they are easygoing, young, salt-of-the-earth Party Chicks. The best acquire that certain edge and become Sexy Feminists; the worst get stuck with a closet twat and become Straight-Pegs ... women who dinnae touch drugs and ... shag only dull twats like themselves who are intae aw that home-and-garden shite.
> WELSH, 1996A

Whatever you make of this male appraisal of modern womanhood, it does illustrate my point that even the most traditional of lads loved what was happening in the genderscape after dark as much as the girls. But it was also this that some reacted against.

CHEMICAL CULTURE AND MODERN MANHOOD

Now some of the capital's clubbers are taking things too far. Way over the top. Now the name of the game is confidence, the courage to be yourself and dress for your fantasies. To be truly fabulous ... The boys can't really take it. They got the leather trousers because of Oliver Stone's The Doors and Primal Scream, but they can't match the girls' attitude. This could be the age of Venus as the femmes take over the floors. If they're not careful, all the boys are going to get is a hefty dose of Venus Envy ... The freedom to flirt is back. It's there to be taken.

MARCUS AND ESHAN, 1991

This article in *Mixmag* magazine was prophetic in some ways. Many a lad didn't or couldn't take up or hold onto the new-found freedom in gender relations on the dancefloor and, as the originally homogeneous Acid House scene perpetually fragmented into scenes defined by different types of dance music, 'hardcore' increasingly became a definition of all things non-girly (largely non-gay and non-black too). Sexed-up irony was for the wimps or the gay boys. Or the way to a quick shag, if you were lucky. Even Manchester's bad boy Shaun Ryder (sensitive after being in drug rehab) showed, in 1992, a preference for a Northern Soul night in Cornwall (because the older punters there just wanted to be going mad, enjoying and loving the music and dancing) to, what he called, the 'deern, deern' of a hardcore night (Balie, 1992). While 'her' version of T-shirts put 'babe power' and 'dolly bird' on the same ironic level in recent times, 'his' version was 'dazed and confused' or 'hardcore'.

LOADED, GOADED OR VENUS ENVY?
MEN SURVIVING

I said earlier that fear of culturE didn't directly pick up on the make-over ladhood was undergoing on the dancefloor. But fear of all this girliness could well have been part of a wider concern about the state of modern manhood. A concern which may well have resulted in the single white female achieving all the public attention when it came to victim status, even though boys have been 'E' casualties too. A concern which also, once we step beyond the drugs and crime moral outrage party, also has room for male victimhood. One the chattering classes on one side of the generational divide call 'the crisis of masculinity'.

You can't turn on the TV or read the paper these days without hearing about it. One day it's sperm counts taking a nose-dive and the Equal Opportunities Commission getting more complaints from men than women about job discrimination and recruitment. The next, it's fathers harassed by the Child Support Agency and boys turning to anorexia like the girls. 'A Bad Time To Be A Man', 'The Men's Ward', 'The Male Survival Guide', 'Men Aren't Working' and 'Women On Men' are now part of an evening in front of the telly. Men are (successfully) committing suicide more (young ones especially), complaining about too much use of the male body as sexual object in advertising and entering a male version of the Miss World beauty competition called Mr UK. They're living at home with their parents much longer, they're opting to live alone and are finding that being free and single is a lonely business. And boys still don't talk about their feelings, a Childline survey informs us, or write to problem pages specializing in soul-baring to cope with it all. Meanwhile women are pinching all the qualifications at school and grabbing all the jobs, while demanding good sex, a good body, good clothes, good housekeeping. Men feel bad about themselves, their relationships, their children, working too hard or not enough. The message is loud and clear.

Or is it? While all this has been going on, we've had the birth of new ladism. Forget the new man of the eighties, all eager to please the girls and no trousers. In the quirky, ironic nineties, his offspring had a much-needed injection of testosterone and forgot male guilt.

Suddenly, football, beer, farts, 'totty' and 'titties' were ironic fun. Men's magazines which, when launched a decade earlier, advised aspiring new men on how to iron a shirt, seemed to get closer and closer to top-shelf soft-porn of the heterosexual kind – led down this path by *Loaded*, the magazine 'for men who should know better'. Suddenly, men behaving badly was vogue.

And, like I said before, I'm the first one to enjoy the irony of playing around with old versions of girl- and boyhood and making them mean something different. And to recognize that the bad lad has always had a lot more woman-appeal than we often care to admit. But like I also said before, it feels like things have gone just that bit too far. 'Suits you sir' accurately describes my ultimate response to an overdose of football and cleavages. And I know I'm not alone or just climbing into bed with the 'no-humour' brigade of both sexes when I say this. The adolescent sexual state, which was the hallmark of ladhood on the 'E' honeymoon in Britain after dark, was one thing. The adolescent state of mainstream masculine culture – from fantasy football to very real lives of crime – is quite another.

Like femininity, masculinity is on the change and we don't know where it's headed. Admitting we're scared is one thing but casting the modern boy either as an evil drug dealing villain or a new-fangled breed altogether lost in music and technology will only give us a false sense of security. Some may be happy to do that. Some may throw up their arms and declare we're all doomed. But I say, Watch This Space. And remember that, in the maelstrom of the post-modern genderscape, culturE has had a role to play. It's not all over yet.

PART 3

The Conclusion

7

Ecstasy: case unsolved

The Ecstasy case is not solved. And it's not really a big deal to say this in Britain in 1996. That much the nation is agreed on. But it's where we go from there that's consistently in dispute. For the official world and for many parents and other people no longer in their youth, the Ecstasy case is a case in need of solving. The future is in danger and the politicians must be seen to take responsibility and offer an effective quick fix, and the medics, policy makers and educationalists must help them find a solution. Meanwhile parents experience very real fear for their children's physical and moral welfare, while the other side of the generational divide just get on with it. Or, at most, view the Ecstasy case largely as one of needing to know more about the drug – its dangers, long-term effects, its content and quality – or one of knowing better than their elders. Either way, the Ecstasy case remains ultimately an open and shut one: quick fix or no fix required.

In true British style, I've examined the British Ecstasy case in isolation (in fact it's even worse than that – it's been largely an English case). That doesn't make me an anti-internationalist, Euro-sceptic or anything else born of living on a small island which still prides itself on past 'ownership' of vast swathes of the planet. It just makes me someone attempting to look at specifics. And although culturE has swept many corners of the world, my line of inquiry at a global level would be a mammoth, if exciting task. So, for now, I've reopened the British Ecstasy case, where the combination of dance, dance music and dance drugs made its way into a specific cultural, economic and political mix of a society over a decade ago. The peculiarly British case of how a mass chemical experiment slotted into the generational dealings, the politics, the cultural forms and identities, and the social class shenanigans of a tiny island.

But I haven't replayed all the old familiar tunes, warm and comforting to all because they either keep the illusion of a quick fix solution alive or entrench the quick fix's flip-side – no fix required. I haven't dedicated text inches to the whys and wherefores of taking a drug, what exactly we know about it, whose information we can trust, who's right or wrong about it, what should be done about it. In reopening the case, I've tried to follow a different line of inquiry. I started from a position of declared uncertainty about it all and invited you to accompany me. I attempted to shift the focus away from the ethical concerns or pharmacology surrounding a drug with the most promising brand name ever and onto its social uses and effects. I have given you a version of the overall state of play in the Ecstasy case in official and popular terms but then I've used my experience as a social researcher, as a girl who grew up in the sixties and as a parent from the seventies to explore how this drug-full-of-promise (of either the positive or negative kind) has been tied up in a whole lot more than we think. And I've done this because the more uncertain I personally become about it all, the more I feel admitting uncertainty is the only way to move beyond the perpetual vicious circle which is the apology for debate on Ecstasy and other illegal drugs in this country.

ECSTASY: CASE UNSOLVED

Let me backtrack; replay what I've been saying. I began by outlining the Ecstasy case so far, the case as it is argued in the public arena. The case which has adults within the official world slogging it out in an eternal cycle of seeming practicality, trading certainties based either on moral outrage or calm rationality. One side aims to banish drugs by saying Just Say No or, more recently, Just Say Know. The other accepts that drugs are here to stay and that the best that can be done is to say Just Say Know the quality of the drug, its effects, how to make things safer, what you don't know. While this public sparring match goes through its stop-go cycle, the ordinary everyday folk just get on with things – usually being afraid on one side of the generational divide and being laid back, on the other.

I suggested ending this cycle for a while, on paper at least, following uncertainty and seeing where it leads us. My new line of inquiry turned our attention to the cultural divide which, I argued, has been a major motor to culturE – the lifestyle gap between the young and the not-so-young, between a world-within-a-world and the official world, between ease and fear. I looked beyond the drug itself and the quest to discover what should be done about it, to what Ecstasy has come to mean over the years on both sides of the generational divide, to the kind of (very different) certainties which have surrounded it. And then, I looked even further, beyond these certainties to what I feel are some of the bigger, more important but yet unsolved social questions which underlie this generational dynamic of which Ecstasy has become symbolic.

ECSTASY – SUBSTANCE OR SUBSTANCES UNKNOWN

First, I illustrated the generational cultural divide by looking at the British adult world's preoccupation with Ecstasy-related death in 1996 on one hand, and the normality of hedonism-in-hard-times in youthful lifestyles, on the other. While accepting the fact that we know very little about Ecstasy, the drug, and could do with knowing more, I also argued that in some ways, knowing more about the drug's long-term effects, toxicity, purity, etc, is a red herring. From what I've seen and the studies tell, the British kids have a great appetite for drugs and knowing more about their harmful effects won't stop it. Like Boy George, pop-star turned DJ and record company boss, suggested at the Guardian 'E' debate in London (to both applause and outrage) recently: 'I think all this information stuff is an excuse. People know the dangers of taking drugs … It's just a way of buying time. We all know that if we take drugs it'll fuck us up … Basically people just hope they don't get damaged by it.' So in some ways, demanding to know more is a smoke screen. An apology for a quick-fix solution. Knowing more about the drug's social effects and uses can tell us rather more.

THE SLIPPERY SLOPE: DRUGS AND DECLINE

Then I moved the inquiry on to the wider question of drugs in general and Ecstasy's central role in how they're perceived on either side of the generational divide. On the one hand, Ecstasy has become the latest in a long line of drugs which spell the doomed fate of a generation. On the other, it has been viewed as unique in its benevolence but, as a result, its reputation helped fuel a youthful penchant for illicit drug-taking like never before. While blanket fear that a drug is a drug is addiction and doom is just plain daft, we need to accept where that fear comes from (mostly but not entirely from little knowledge of illicit drug-taking cultures). We also need to distinguish between the very different cultures surrounding the use of different drugs. Shooting up heroin in a squat is a world away from dancing the night away on Ecstasy. But more than that there is the difference between taking drugs to enhance the good things and taking drugs to escape the bad ... for a long time. Any drug, yes legal ones too, can be used for this purpose and they frequently are. But we have no way of predicting how many of the new chemical generation will take up running away through drug-taking as a major lifestyle option which dwarfs all others – long-term. We only have past youth drug cultures in consumer society to go on. And, although their obvious casualties may have been few, the feel-good factor in society and the economy as a whole then was that much better than it is now. CulturE has its casualties already but they currently appear to be a minority right now. Only time will tell the eventual outcome for a drug-taking culture of excess.

ECSTASY AND THE POST-MODERN GENDERSCAPE

Finally, I looked beyond the question of drug-taking per se to the impact of the cultures which have grown up around dance, dance music and dance drugs on youthful identity and on the adult world's perception of it. I focussed on gender because it has been a big subject in my research work. But I also happen to think that culturE has provided an important arena for working through new gender identities, new twists to the male/female dynamic. Something the official world has refused to acknowledge in public debate but which, I suspect, underlies much of its fear of or antagonism towards culturE. While the official world has fretted about the single white female as culturE's innocent victim and laid most of the blame firmly at the door of (in an unusual move away from blaming black men for crime) white males, something has been happening to what little boys and girls are made of. While the official world has seen nothing but a traditional girl, upright and true to the last of all things normal, and a boy who is the perpetrator of all things asocial – villainous, self-centred, violent and criminal – there's been a lot more afoot in the world-within-a-world of the new chemical culture. Girls who had benefited from the new settlement between the sexes afforded by high male unemployment, low male self-esteem and the drip of the feminist tap into mainstream popular culture, took to the new nocturnal social space in a big way. As punters, they loved what the combination of a drug, a type of music and social setting like never before did to relations between the sexes in Britain after dark.

It gave them power. Power to revel in their own sensuality and sexuality, to conduct their relationships with the boys on their own terms. Power to be social in a way they'd never known before. Power to express their emotions and feelings without worrying about the consequences, to hug someone – male or female – on impulse; and for it not to matter. Power to work a crowd through their body movements and facial expressions if the feeling took them. And, to begin with, the boys loved it too. It was liberating to roam in this girly world of physicality, sensuality and emotion, especially for the white, straight boys. A sort of football experience (all social belonging, emotion and roaring) with the testosterone taken out and the closest you'd want to get to religion thrown in. But the boy punters didn't stay all girly and united, didn't stay just punters for long. The days when football love-thug, black and gay boys were among many versions of ladhood dancing, hugging and massaging each other en masse, were limited. Many got uncomfortable and went their separate ways. Meanwhile there were those who didn't just want to be made to dance by someone else. They wanted to be the man up there in control of the crowd. Or the man selling the drugs, or organizing the event. Leaving the girls … where exactly? Feeling like a great opportunity had been missed more than anything, I suspect. Back to dancing with other girls and gay boys, like they had before culturE ever happened. Back to the gay clubs which had played such a formative role in dance culture. But that's where I should butt my aging body out of things. It's just an old duffer's version of a gender story which will take a long time in the full unravelling.

I have to say I find it odd, in some ways, that an official world obsessed with solving the law and order question (which had delivered Thatcherism unto the nation but which refused to go away) did not respond positively to a youth culture which took its unemployed youth, its football hooligans off the streets and transformed them into creative love and peace merchants and even operated a successful job creation scheme of its own, leaving the market to respond positively instead. Ok, so all of the jobs weren't exactly legal and there's the rub. Along with the fact that the testosteroned-up parliamentary system and guardians of the old world order must have found it hard to swallow the idea of men of all social and sexual persuasions dancing together, Luving and pleasuring each other even. Social mixing of the really threatening kind perhaps?

THERE'S SOMETHING HAPPENING HERE BUT I DON'T KNOW WHAT IT IS

Anyway, I wanted to take a peek beyond a drug called Ecstasy to its conceptual and cultural consumption in Britain and I took a fresh look at the key fears publicly expressed about the drug to do this. Gender has been central to the voicing of public fears and I've focussed on that subject to illustrate what happens if you follow my new line of inquiry. You see a society on the change (so what's new?) and you see culturE as both a product of and vehicle for that change. But just where it's all headed is still up for grabs.

Given time and word space, it would have been good to give other areas of social identity and change relating to culturE the same treatment. To carry on the investigation. And to look behind the white heterosexual image of culturE in the official world at how black and gay club culture shaped it in Britain but in turn got significantly changed by it, for a time at least. Or to look at how fear on one side of the generational divide can cast much of tomorrow's youth as 'raving mad', while the other side consider altered mind states a normal part of life, a positive lifestyle attribute, a reason to be psychically superior to 'straight' society, or a right even. Or to give more detail still to the amorphous mass of 'youth' and look at the impact of dance culture on different age groups. Talking about 18 to 35 year olds and chemical culture is one thing. Talking about the under 15s, especially, is another. Design, technology, cyber- and virtual space are all important aspects of culturE which I've hardly mentioned. Thinking about the young people who define themselves against it, proclaim 'it's great when you're straight' and continue to do so after they've turned 16, is something we really need to explore (especially when sport, religion and other seeming cultural antidotes don't necessarily seem to guarantee culturE immunity). And then, of course, there's politics.

PARTY POLITICS

Until quite recently I would have been writing a very different book. I would have jumped on the certainty bandwagon and tried to shock at least half the population into getting real about a generation's lifestyle in the uncertainty and decadence at the end of a century. I wouldn't have been saying Just Say Stop and Think. I'd have been saying, do something about it. Stop all the hypocritical pronouncing on a generation in a fix. Stop sipping pints and glasses of wine, stop downing tranquillizers and sleeping pills, stop dealing with your anxiety about your own and your nearest and dearest lives, about the future (of Britain and the human race) with state-sponsored chemicals while denouncing the chemical solutions of another generation. Stop the hypocrisy and, if you're really concerned adults, take some real responsibility. I certainly wouldn't have been saying Watch This Space. I would have shouted out a solution of some kind.

And politics would have played a significant part in that solution. I didn't get parliamentary politics (yes I did join the Labour Party when Maggie came to power), after years of trying, à la David Bowie, to ignore the establishment to death for nothing. I didn't join the political club in order to oust what I thought was the biggest threat to the British welfare state since it was born, to pass the time. I didn't believe in politics with a small 'p', the ability to fight for what your identity said was right, to sit back and watch a generation devoted to defining their identities through pleasure and a range of responses to the established order of total dedication to material wealth, rationality and sod the rest, castigated. I certainly didn't think I'd been through all the castigation of my own youthful yearning for a more fulfilling sense of belonging, of community, of self-help and -reliance, a more fulfilling life goal than the suburban dream of a nine-to-five income and comfortable reproduction of the race, to abandon it entirely and damn a generation for wanting what seemed spookily similar.

But actually, like many wrinklies these days as well as the young, I find it hard to have faith in traditional politics as the vehicle of change. Or at least, Westminster, political parties, trade unions no longer feel like a convincing way to really get the society we dream of. In fact, the goal of achieving a half-way decent society seems to have gone down the pan in the minds of many citizens during a long feel-bad-factor era. Club 18–34 (7 million men and 7 million women) now make up a third of the voting population but nearly half of 18 to 25 year olds didn't vote in the last election and 1 in 5 of them do not register to vote (four times more than the rest of the population). Politics is as crazy and mixed up as any adolescent.

So my line of inquiry into politics and culturE would have to be based on as much uncertainty as the rest of it has been. But Politics with a capital 'P' is where my generational divide to the investigation would have to stop. Not a lot of the population as a whole on all sides have much faith in it any more. The divide is between them and the official world. Instead of waiting for an ideal political heaven, many folk of all ages appear to have left the political institutions and languages of old behind entirely. Conservative versus Labour? Forget it. Radical or conservative? Means nothing to many these days. Now it's largely a matter of concern, but cynicism and apathy or single issue politics – where mixed bands of individuals tussle with corporate culture to save the planet or the animals, or where establishing a particular social identity becomes a reason for banding together. Road protests and demonstrations against animal exports now unite middle-class, cat-owning pensioners and boys with a full set of tattoos and body piercings. Meanwhile, fighting for the Right To Party has united many of the youth who never got political before with those still burning from the Poll Tax. And, however puny or pathetic the stalwarts of old forms of macho politics may declare it (just the kind of self-indulgence you would expect from the Me generation brought up on greed and materialism), it's a sign of the times. Times when the state feels irrelevant but also highly intrusive to many young people – on the one hand offering and providing very little but stepping in with the heaviest of hands to police the very things (some feel) they have left.

IT'S GREAT WHEN YOU'RE STRAIGHT: THE THIN END OF THE GENERATIONAL WEDGE

So the Ecstasy case is not solved. And it's not solved in all kinds of ways we haven't begun to even think about very hard. Just Say Think is a bit of a pathetic thing to shout. Just Say Watch This Space even worse. There's not much doing, not much solving in it. And it sounds like a very rational thing to do about a cultural phenomenon so based on irrationality and about the irrational responses it has provoked in the world outside it (the very rational response of legal and illegal private markets excepted). I'm the last one to believe in the punch a dose of rationality can pack these days. But I suppose I prefer it to apportioning blame willy nilly. Don't get me wrong, a good old slagging-off session does me as much good as anyone else. But in the end, like it or not, offering no solutions is actually my contribution to the Ecstasy case. It's time we either buried it (but that seems increasingly impossible) or posed some different questions instead.

And one of the biggest questions, from where I stand, is can the current dynamic of the generational divide around drugs and lifestyle, the one that's been so central a factor in it all, survive? The one which has journalist Mary Kenny voicing the thoughts of many over the generational Ecstasy hill, in a debate on Ecstasy on the BBC's *Heart of the Matter* programme, when she says:

> Drugs culture is actually a refusal to experience life ... to actually feel and taste and know life. We live in a culture which is premised on instant gratification. I want the drug to give me happiness now. Human psychology isn't like that. Happiness is something that happens to you because you're doing something interesting or with someone you love ... It's an artificial world which is rejecting real experience.

... while, in the next breath, eulogising about the creative, intellectual and very real nature of a drink in the pub. The cultural divide which has the bereaved parents of Leah Betts doing their best to make things OK for other ordinary parents and saying:

> We don't think we're the only parents in the land that never realized just what a youth culture this is. Had we known that we could have said to Leah, look we know this is part of your way of enjoying yourself, the same way we used to go out and have a half a lager but can we talk about this. You explain to us, tell us what it's all about.
>
> JANET BETTS ON *PUBLIC EYE* 'BEYOND THE DRUGS WAR' BBC2, MARCH 1996

ECSTASY: CASE UNSOLVED

This is a brave attempt at understanding but so far from the mark, it feels. The social order these parents are harking back to, where 'going out for a half of lager' to enjoy yourself was still one of relatively few consumer leisure options for the young has been radically transformed. The home you went out of, or escaped from was something you expected to replace with one of your own after a brief period of sowing the wild oats of youth. The pub you went out to was still, although long in decline, a cornerstone of popular culture. A form of leisure you engaged in after finishing work. 'Work, rest and play' were the social order of the majority's day – even if you chose to rebel against it. The world you went about your daily business in had (at least the whiff of) a feel-good factor. Now there's a feel-bad factor in the general atmosphere, home is something large numbers of people stay in all day, work is something many spend their time trying to get, resting and playing are either too much or too little of an option and there's little shared rhythm to the day or to life in general. And illegal drugs have been incorporated into real life for many under 35 years of age, as well as into forms of escape well intent on being permanent.

The generational divide is so big that even the hours people of different generations keep are often out of sync. The big wigs in the drinks industry, beleaguered by dwindling sales among the young, called in young consultants and found to their horror that they were harbouring 'underwolves' in their very own homes, teens so-called by the authors of a report by the think tank, Demos, on their survey of September 1995. *Harpers and Queen* warned us that 'The Nineties have produced a new breed of adolescent. Idle, apathetic and devoid of ambition, the Underwolf only comes out at night – to eat cornflakes, watch videos and take drugs. Check that darkened room', we were told. 'An untamed species closely related to you', active from dusk 'til dawn, lacking in interest in getting on and acquiring the values of parents, was now official, typifying the characteristics of more than half of under 25s – who, according to the Demos report, feel disconnected from the political system, patriotism and the discipline of older people, and what was more, the figures said they would remain so (Barr, 1996).

This divide sees more and more studies which tell us of a 'lost generation' of half a million unemployed under 25 year olds. A generation which a 'disconnection index', recently prepared by Socioconsult (part of MORI), showed that 54 per cent of 18 to 24 year olds are proud not to be part of the British system, as compared with 37 per cent of 25 to 34 year olds; 28 per cent of 35 to 44 olds; 18 per cent of 45 to 54 olds; 15 per cent of 55 to 64 olds; and 8 per cent of 65 year olds and over. A generation in which there has been a big rise in suicide, crime, depression, alcohol and substance abuse, anorexia and bulimia; seen educational standards under fire, juvenile crime on the increase, drugs increasingly prevalent within, as well as beyond, the school gates. A generation which has seen a growth in youth markets and culture which marks them off as a separate group more than ever before; and, at the same time, a lengthening of youth and postponement of economic independence. A generation which has been variously described as, in terms American, 'the slacker generation' or 'generation X'; in terms Euro, the 'MTV generation'; in terms British, the 'Me' generation or 'Thatcher's children'. And yet, a generation among which, we are told, 80 per cent of 18 to 22 year olds are optimistic about their future – more than any other group. A generation the tail end of which, or perhaps the full-stop to which, the survey which supplemented the British Social Attitudes report (annual benchmark of how we think and feel), for the first time, also tells us 'young people like things pretty much as they are, know the difference between right and wrong, and tend to believe in God' (Roberts and Sachdev, 1996). This survey was conducted among 12 to 19 year olds, the ones who hadn't left home at the time of interview.

ECSTASY: CASE UNSOLVED

The cultural divide gets the grown-ups blaming their offspring for not getting on in life, for being sluggish and idle but, nonetheless, sees them worried about their offspring to such a degree that a MORI poll commissioned by Barnardos found, in summer 1995, that almost 2 in 3 adults believe today's children have a worse deal than when they were kids; that 7 out of 10 adults believe kids are more aware of issues like poverty and homelessness and 9 out of 10 believe their offspring will witness more violence and crime than a generation ago. And this not just among the middle classes who supposedly read and worry more than the rest. The cultural divide sees grown-ups looking at today's pre-pubescents and worrying about the destruction of innocent childhood: through crime, child murder, child abuse, media overload, sex information overdose and consumer sophistication which sees kids distinguishing between 40 pairs of trainers; sees adults watching or reading about Larry Clarke's film, *Kids*, in Britain in May 1996 – a film about sex-crazed, drug-addled teens behaving badly – worrying about whether they're typical of a generation; but also sees 84 per cent of young people between the ages of 11 and 15 years respecting their parents more than anyone else, according to an ICM poll conducted for *The Guardian* (*The Guardian*, 1996).

Angels, devils or just kids? The summer of 1992, which saw 'Toytown Techno' rave tracks sampling children's TV themes such as 'Sesame Street' and 'A Trip To Trumpton' crossing over into the mainstream, was just one sign that tomorrow's generation wants to hold onto some kind of notion of childhood innocence. But how different is that from an older generation, the majority of whom pine for the security and the old world order of the fifties 'Never Had it So Good' years of their youth or prime? Or from those comic bit-part players in the nineties drugs melodrama, the youth of yesteryear, who pine for or mourn the loss of the days when taking drugs, growing your hair and wearing something other than a suit spelled nothing but a revolution?

ECSTASY: CASE UNSOLVED

So, I'll ask the question which may prove to be the ultimate social solution to the Ecstasy case, regardless of what other solutions may be proposed in the meantime, again: can the current dynamic of the generational divide around drugs and lifestyle survive? I can only answer from the perspective of being one of the breed who didn't just go out for a half of lager to enjoy themselves. Of a girl who grew up in the sixties and whose subsequent personal and working life has not been divorced from youth drug cultures. Like I said before, I'm not exactly Absolutely Fabulous. I may still have a hedonistic bent, given the chance, but I combine it with a good old-fashioned work ethic. I don't fetishize all things youthful while actively disliking young people. I don't think my own or many other people's offspring are boring. Quite the contrary. What is more, I'm part of a growing breed. One growing so much, in fact, that, like it or not, there will soon be a Planet Middle Age on which those who have had some kind of experience of illicit drug cultures in a consumer society (and the solutions and values they provide the young) will be in a majority (even if, like US President Clinton, they didn't inhale). Quite what kind of society they'll be parenting is hard to imagine (although some of them are already doing it, of course). But one thing's for sure. They will inherit the earth, no matter how much we blame them, pity them, or empathize with them. In the end, we, the generations over the Ecstasy hill, haven't delivered a wonderful society for them, no matter what our politics or non-politics have been. In the end, no amount of guilty hand-wringing, arrogant finger-pointing or just plain ignoring them will matter. They'll just have to get on with it. And they are already, in the ways they know how.

I began this book by saying I was an aspiring interpreter of wrinkly twat and twaddle. It's a fundamentally limited and possibly misguided pursuit but I've done what I can. I've attempted to seize on the partial lifting of the veil between the generations brought about by the death of Leah Betts in the home of her normal, everyday parents in late 1995, to look at the Ecstasy case from both sides and move beyond them. Admitting uncertainty wasn't easy for me. For me, it's all too easy to give in to adult angst and dismiss everything but the fear, on one hand. It's all too easy to go with the flow of things youthful and say drugs, sex and music, so what, on the other. It's also all too easy to follow a professional career and declare we must say this or that. But it's worth noting that I have had all these things to push me into certainty and I've still come out saying I personally just don't know any more. Uncertainty is probably something which will never reach any of the powerful parts that matter in the Ecstasy case. And I don't expect for a minute that sending out a shout in small book form will change the social need to trade in certainties. But it may change a few of the old tunes of public discussion just a little. Get them out of the groove they're stuck in. For now Just Say Think.

Bibliography

Anonymous (1991) Letters Page, *The Face*, November.

Arlidge, J. (1994) 'Slaughter By The Needle', *The Independent*, May 8: 9.

Balie, S. (1992) 'Repent Boys', *New Musical Express*, October 17: 14–15 and 61.

Barr, A. (1996) 'The Company Of Underwolves', *Harpers and Queen*, January: 70–75.

Bellos, A. (1995) 'The Buddha Of Euphoria', *The Guardian*, April 6: 4.

Bennetto, J. (1994) 'Drug Abuse Lays Waste A Generation', *The Independent On Sunday*, May 8: front page.

Benson, R. (1996) 'Over The Rainbow', *The Face*, March: 86–90.

Brindle, D. (1996) 'Drugs Fear For Under–11s', *The Guardian*, January 31: 2.

Buffum, J. and Moser, C. (1986) 'MDMA And Sexual Function', *Journal of Psychoactive Drugs*, 18, 4 (October–December): 353–9.

Bunting, M. (1994) 'Drugs Advice Hard To Find', *The Guardian*, June 6: 2.

Campbell, B. (1996) 'Girls On Safari', *The Guardian*, July 15: 4–5.

Campbell, D. (1994) 'Strong-Arm Men', *The Guardian*, March 23: 12.

Carroll, C. (1992) 'Girls Don't Count' in *The Sol Mix. Manchester Music and Design 1976–1992*, Manchester, Cornerhouse Exhibitions.

Champion, S. (1990) *And God Created Manchester*, Manchester, Wordsmith.

Cohen, J. (1996) 'Drugs In The Classroom. Politics, Propaganda And Censorship', *Druglink*, 11, 2, March/April: 12–13.

Coffield, F. and Gofton, L. (1994) *Drugs and Young People*, London, Institute for Public Policy Research.

Collard, J. (1995) 'How Safe Are Your Drugs?', *Real Life. Independent On Sunday*, November 19: 3.

Collins, J. (1996) *The Sex We Want. Straight Talking From 90's Women*, London, Pandora.

Corrigan, S. (1995) 'Heroin Sells Even As It Kills', *i-D*, 146, November: 64–7.

Costello, J. (1985) *Love, Sex And War. Changing Values 1939–45*, London, Collins.

Creed, T. (1993) *Social Interactions At Raves: A Raver's/Sociologist's Study*, Manchester, 'University of Madchester'.

Daily Express (1988) 'Drug Mother's Anguish', November 1.

Daily Star (1988) 'Dicing With A Cocktail Of Death', November 2.

Daily Star (1992) 'What A Dope!', January 29: front page.

Derges, J. (1996) 'Lara's Message', *Eastern Daily Express*, March 25: 11.

Dixon, S. (1993) 'Has The Nightmare Begun?', *Mixmag*, 2, 21, February: 16–18.

DJ (1994) 'DJ Profile', March 31–April 13: 24.

Dorn, N. and Murji, K. (1992) *Drug Prevention: A Review Of The English Language Literature*, London, Institute for the Study of Drug Dependence.

Edwards, J. and Midgley, C. 'I Sold E At Coma Girl's Club', *Daily Mirrror*, November 14: front page.

Eimer, D. (1993) 'Britain: A Country On The Blag?', *i-D. The Survival Issue*, February: 35–6.

Ennett, S. et al (1994) 'How Effective Is Drug Abuse Resistance Education?', *American Journal of Public Health*, 84, 9.

Everitt, P. (1986) 'You'll Never Be 16 Again. An Illustrated History Of The Teenager, BBC Publications.

Field, K. (1992) 'Famous Last Words. E Youth Mind F**K', Mixmag, 2, 10, March: 58.

Fiske, J. (1989) Reading The Popular: Madonna. London, Routledge.

Forsyth, J. (1995) 'Ecstasy And Illegal Drug Use Design: A New Concept In Drug Use', The International Journal On Drug Policy, 6, 3: 193–209.

Fossier, A.E. (1931) 'The Marijuana Menace', New Orleans Medical And Surgical Journal, 84, October, quoted in Mandel, J. (1968) 'Who Says Marijuana Use Leads To Addiction?', Journal Of Secondary Education, 43, 5: 211–17.

Friend, M. (1994) 'Country Pursuits', The Guardian, February 16: 12–13.

Generator (1994) 'Rachel Auburn. On Drugs, Clubs, The Crowd And Her Handbag Of Delights...', 13, Summer.

Gilman, M. (1992) 'No More Junkie Heroes', Druglink, 7, 3: 16.

Gilman, M. (1993) 'Harm Reduction And The New Puritans'. Paper to the IVth International Conference on the Reduction of Drug Related Harm, Rotterdam, The Netherlands, March.

Graham, J. and Bowling, B. (1996) Young People And Crime, London, Home Office Research Study.

Hadfield, C. (1992) 'Ecstasy Agony Of The TV Flake Girl', Daily Mirror, November 1.

Harpin, L. (1992) 'DJ Of The Month', i-D, 104, May: 64.

Hawthorne, G. et al (1995) 'Does Life Education's Drug Education Programme Have A Public Benefit?', Addiction, 90.

Headon, J. (1996a) 'One Foot In The Rave', Mixmag, 2, 56: 60–4.

Headon, J. (1996b) 'Too Young To Die', Mixmag, 2, 56: 72–4.

Health Education Authority (1996) Drug Realities – National Drugs Campaign Survey. London, HEA.

Henderson, S. (1993a) Young Women, Sexuality And Recreational Drug Use: Final Report, Manchester, Lifeline Project.

Henderson, S. (1993b) 'Time For A Make-over', Druglink, September/October: 14–16.

Henderson, S. (1993c) 'Keep Your Bra And Burn Your Brain?', Druglink, November/December: 10–12.

Henderson, S. (1993d) 'Luvdup and Deeelited: Responses To Drug Use In The Second Decade' in Aggleton, P., Davies, P. and Hart, G. (eds) AIDS: Facing the Second Decade, London, Falmer Press.

Hodgkinson, T. (1996) 'Who Takes And Eats?', The Guardian, November 17: 21

Holland, J., Ramazanoglu, C. and Scott, S. (1990) Sex, Risk And Danger. AIDS Education Policy And Young Women's Sexuality, WRAP Paper 1. London, Tufnell Press.

Horton, P. (1986) 'Calling Card Of A Deadly Salesman ...', South Wales Echo, January 18.

Hudson, C. (1994) 'Just Who Is Mrs Woods?', apn Magazine, 46, August.

James, M. (1991) 'Drug Bores', The Face 42: 123

Johnston, L. (1995–6) 'Smack Is Back', The Big Issue, 161, December 18–January 1: 8–13.

Kohn, M. (1992) Dope Girls. The Birth of the British Drug Underground, London, Lawrence and Wishart.

Leisure Consultants (1990) Leisure Trends: The Thatcher Years. Leisure Consultants.

Liverpool Echo (1992) 'Raving Mad', January 28.

Marcus, T. and Eshan, K. (1991) 'Fabulous', Mixmag, 2, 6, December: 34.

McDermott, P. (1991) 'Legal Highs', The Face, 49, October: 109.

McDermott, P., Matthews, A. and O'Hare, P. (1993) 'Ecstasy In The UK: Recreational Drug Use And Cultural Change' in Heather, N., Wodak, A., Nadelmann, E. and O'Hare, P. (eds) Psychoactive Drugs And Harm Reduction. From Faith To Science, London, Whurr.

Mixmag (1992) Editorial, 2, 16.

Mixmag (1993) 'What Would You Do With A Million Pounds?', 2, 25, July: 10–11.

Mixmag (1994) 'Fashion Splesh', 2, 35, April: 3.

Mixmag (1996a) 'Aging Ravers Become Club Celebs', 2, 59, April: 16.

Mixmag (1996b) 'Clubbers Confess Sex Antics', 2, 56, January: 16.

Moore, S. (1996) 'Takin' Out My Generation', The Guardian, May 16: 5.

Moriarty, F. (ed) (1979) True Confessions. 1919–1979. Sixty Years Of Sin, Suffering And Sorrow, New York, Simon and Schuster.

Nasmyth, P. (1985) 'Ecstasy (MDMA)', *The Face*, 66: 88–93.

Nasmyth, P. (1986) 'The Agony And The Ecstasy', *The Face*, 78: 53–5.

Nelson, D. (1994) 'Free Will Versus The Slavery Of Addiction', *The Observer*, August 14: 18.

Neustatter, A. (1996) 'Mid-Life Crisis? You're Not Alone', *The Guardian* 2, January 8: 2–5.

Offbeat (1988) 'Who Killed Smiley?', 2, October.

Parker, H., Measham, F. and Aldridge, J. (1995) *Drug Futures. Changing Patterns Of Drug Use Among English Youth*, London, ISDD.

Pragnell, M. (1988) 'The Summer Of Acid House Hype', *The Sunday Times*, October 30.

Ramsay, M. and Percy, A. (1996) *Drug Misuse Declared: Results Of The 1994 British Crime Survey*, London, Home Office.

Redhead, S. (ed) *Rave Off: Politics and Deviance In Contemporary Youth Culture*, Aldershot, Avebury.

Roberts, H. and Sachdev, D. (eds) (1996) *Young People's Social Attitudes*, London, Barnardos in collaboration with Social and Community Planning Research.

Sarler, C. (1994) 'Love Pilgrim's Progress', *The Guardian*, 28 July.

Shapiro, H. 'Heroin In The '90s: From A To B', *Druglink*, 11, 3, May/June: 8–9.

Silva, G. (1979) *The Dope Chronicles. 1850–1950*, San Francisco, Harper and Row.

Silvester, N. (1996) 'Trail Of Evil Psycho', *Sunday Mail*, May 26: front page.

Smash Hits (1992) Front Cover and 'Get Sorted', October 14–27: 15–19.

Stall, R., McKusick, L., Wiley, J., Coates, T. and Ostrow, D. (1986) 'Alcohol And Drug Use During Sexual Activity And Compliance With Safe Sex Guidelines', *Health Education Quarterly*, 13: 359–71.

Stall, R. (1988) 'The Prevention Of HIV Infection Associated With Drug And Alcohol Use During Sexual Activity', in Siegel, L. (ed) *AIDS And Substance Abuse*, New York, Harington Park Press.

Stern, C. (1996) 'Killer Drugs Flood Back', *The Mail On Sunday*, February 4: 23.

Stone, C. (1996) *Fierce Dancing*, London, Faber and Faber.

Sunday Mirror (1993) 'Would You Believe It? Rave Review For Cinders', January 10.

Sweeney, J. (1996) 'Barbarism Behind Murder Of Leah', *Daily Mail*, June 8: 22–3.

The Guardian (1996) 'Kids', May 14 and 15.

The People (1988) 'Dodgy Roger, The Acid House King', December 11: 9.

The Sun (1988) 'Acid Fiend Spikes Page Three Girl's Drink', November 24.

The Sun (1992) 'Fury At Sex Guide To "E" ', January 29: front page.

Thompson, D. (1994) 'Jobs For The Boys', *DJ*, 15–28 September: 36–7.

Thornton, S. (1995) *Club Cultures. Music, Media And Subcultural Capital*, London, Polity Press.

Travis, A. (1996) 'Heroin Dealers Target "Lucrative" UK', *The Guardian*, March 19: 5.

Twomey, J. (1988) 'Peril Of New Love Drug', *The Daily Express*, November 3.

Wade, N. (1969) 'Pot And Heroin', *New Society*, January 22: 117–18.

Welsh, I. (1995) *Marabou Stork Nightmares*, London, Jonathan Cape.

Welsh, I. (1996a) *Ecstasy*, London, Jonathan Cape.

Welsh, I. (1996b) 'City Tripper', *The Guardian*, February 16: 4.

Whittow, H. and Edwards, J. (1988) 'Dicing With A Cocktail Of Death', *Daily Star*, November 2.

Williams, M. (1988) 'Blasphemy. Nothing Is Sacred To This Warped Drug Cult', *The Post*, November 14: front page.

Wootton, B. (1969) 'Cannabis Is Not Heroin', *Science Journal*, 5A, 3: 3.

Yates, R. (1992) *If It Weren't For The Alligators. A History Of Drugs, Music And Popular Culture In Manchester*, Manchester, The Lifeline Project.